# A Black Country Mixture

Extracts from the Blackcountryman
by Stan Hill

The Black Country Society

July 2009

ISBN 978-0-904015-80-5

Prepared for publication by Tim Cockin at Malthouse Press, Grange
Cottage, Malthouse Lane, Barlaston, Staffordshire, ST12 9AQ

Cover design by Malthouse Press
after the original design by
The Charles Group, Kingswinford


Printed by Lightning Source Ltd.

# Contents

# WHAT IS THE BLACK COUNTRY

The term 'The Black Country' was first used in the mid 19th century to describe the area on the South Staffordshire Coalfield, where the 'thick coal' lay. The 1850s and 1860s saw the peak of mineral and iron production and the area would have been at its blackest then.

Over 150 square miles some 100 small industrial communities developed and by the turn of the century a couple of dozen of them were of sufficient size, perhaps when linked with some of their neighbours, to have their own municipal councils.

There were never any precise boundaries for the Black Country for the term was not official, not to be found on Ordnance Survey maps, for example. However, 20 years campaigning by the Black Country Society and others, seemed to bear fruit regarding the name, for in 1987, the Government sponsored body 'The Black Country Development Corporation' was established with a 10 year life, later extended by one year. What was once a nickname was elevated to be included to describe an official body.

By 1974 all the townships of the Black Country, by whatever definition, were absorbed into four Black Country Metropolitan Boroughs; further official acceptance of the name.

# THE BLACK COUNTRY SOCIETY

This voluntary society was founded in 1967 as a reaction to the trend of the 1950s and early 1960s to amalgamate everything into large units and in the Midlands to sweep away the area's industrial heritage in the process.

The general aim of the Society is to create interest in the past, present and future of the Black Country, and early on it campaigned for the establishment of an industrial museum. In 1975 the Black Country Living Museum was started by Dudley Borough Council on 26 acres of totally derelict land adjoining the grounds of Dudley Castle. This has developed into an award-winning museum which attracts over 200,000 visitors annually.

In 1998 the Museum Board secured a lottery grant of nearly £3 million towards the £4.5 million cost of building a state-of-the-art interpretation centre. Known as the Rolfe Street Baths Project as it incorporated that Smethwick building which was transferred to the museum site, it was officially opened on 18 May 2001. It includes two fine exhibition halls, administration and storage rooms and retains the original Victorian building's facade. The museum's already wide range of attractions is likely soon to be increased in the field of transport with the acquisition of two major collections of vehicles.

At the Black Country Living Museum there is a boat dock fully equipped to restore narrowboats of wood and iron and different vessels can be seen on the dock throughout the year. From behind the Bottle and Glass Inn visitors can travel on a canal boat into Dudley Canal Tunnel, a memorable journey to see spectacular limestone caverns and the fascinating Castle Mill Basin.

There are over 2,000 members of the Black Country Society and all receive the quarterly magazine The Blackcountryman, of which 146 issues have been published since its founding in 1967. In the whole collection there are some 2,000 authoritative articles on all aspects of the Black Country by historians, teachers, researchers, students, subject expects and ordinary folk with an extraordinary story to tell. The whole constitutes a unique resource about the area and is a mine of information for students and researchers who frequently refer to it. Many schools and libraries are subscribers. Over 2,000 copies of the magazine are printed each quarter. It is non-commercial, and contributors do not receive payment for their articles.

# Foreword

Without doubt Stan Hill is a stalwart of The Black Country Society. He has worked hard for the Society over many decades, for their magazine as contributor, editor and latterly as the Advertisements, Distribution and Publications Officer, but in a wider sense, too, he has significantly raised the profile of the Black Country. In June 2007 Stan was deservedly awarded the British Association of Local History's Personal Achievement in Local History Award for his efforts.

I cannot remember the moment I first met Stan but it would be before the publication of my *Staffordshire Encyclopaedia* in 2000. I shall never forget he and Jean managed to make it to Stafford for the launch of the book, coming from the farthest corner of old Staffordshire. Since then, time and time again, Stan has given me break after break (sometimes covertly!) with publishing opportunities and promoting the work I do, for which I am eternally grateful.

This is the second of two books completed for him this year. There was to be one book known as *A Black Country Miscellany*, but it was spotted here really lay two books! One constituted a follow-on to *57 Black Country People* (*57 More Black Country People* came out in the summer), whilst the other constituted a mixture of material which would make another sort of book. This is that book. Each section is given over to every aspect of the magazine which Stan had a hand in. I have modelled the cover on a particular Blackcountryman cover from Stan's formative years as editor, he sent me. It is Winter, 1994, volume 27 No. 1, and the price then was £1.00.

Proudly stapled to the inside cover of his copy is a note from Robert Fellows, Private Secretary to The Queen, from Sandringham House. It is dated 30th December 1993 and thanks Stan for sending The Queen his profile of Harry Eccleston, engraver to the Royal Mint, born Coseley 1923. Her Majesty read the profile with much interest, and asked to express her gratitude to Stan for his thoughtfulness in sending it to her. You will remember Harry's portrait of The Queen adorned bank notes whilst his drawings of famous Britons adorned the reverse sides.

iii

There is another reason which makes Stan cherish this issue, and is an extraordinary coincidence. On page 34 there is a short article about Harts Hill 'Bus Garage, Brierley Hill. A man walks in the foreground, and a young couple are caught in the distance looking into a shop window. Believe it or not the couple looking into the Midland Red Office window for details of their coach trips is Stan and Jean, the year before they were married. They don't know who took the photograph.

I hope you enjoy this book as much as I have putting it together. It is a worthy tribute to a man - or should that be mon - who has given so much to the promotion of the history and culture of his native region. Thank you Stan.

Tim Cockin, Barlaston, 2009.

# Introduction

Upon becoming Editor of *The Blackcountryman* in 1988 I started on a series of profiles, 'Black Country Personalities' and included one in each of the next 75 issues. In 2002 the Black Country Society published *57 Black Country People* a compilation of the first 57 of these articles. The follow up *57 More Black Country People* appeared earlier this year.

For the hundredth issue of *The Blackcountryman* (Volume 25 Number 4, October 1992), the late Harold Parsons (Editor 1967–1988) wrote a brief history of the Black Country Society. To bring this history up to date a perusal of the selection of my Editorials between 1988 and 2001 may be helpful for they give a glimpse of the building up of the Society from a base of about 1,000 members to over 2,000 in 1993 and 2,700 in 2001, and how a wide range of new initiatives contributed to this expansion.

Membership recruitment was greatly helped by the Committee's decision to release some 25,000 back issues of the magazine held in store, in sets of the first 80 magazines for £10, plus a membership subscription.

The Editorials summarise some of the events organised by the Committee to publicise the Society and widen its scope, and draw attention to particular matters, such as the preparation of a 'Conspectus' (22/1), the special issue of the magazine to cover the National Canal Boat Rally at Bumblehole, Netherton (24,2), refuting the suggestion of the Chairman of the English Tourist Board that the term 'The Black Country' should be dropped (24/3), organising local history fairs at Dudley

Town Hall (25/2) and a Black Country Society day at the Black Country Living Museum (27/1), the first book in the Sutton Publishing series on the Black Country, *Wednesbury in Old Photographs*, by Ian Bott, (28/1), other successful publications (28/1), achieving a membership of 2,000 (26/3), defending the term 'The Black Country' (31/3), Black Country Local History Fair at Dudley Town Hall (31/4), the Lisa Potts GM story (34/1 and 34/2), 'signing off' as Editor (34/2).

In the 'Flying the Flag' section which follows the Editorials, are further reports about publicising the Society.

The Black Country Society's activities have received excellent coverage by *The Express & Star* and our association with that company in joint publications, books, and two calendars (2000 and 2001), was most successful. Our own list of books published increased considerably and several long established titles, *Black Country Stories,* (1968, 11 impressions since), and *Black Country Humour,* (1980, 9 impressions since), have achieved sales in excess of 30,000. In addition the Society has published over 20 more serious titles, usually with an initial print run of 2,000.

In 1994, Sutton Publishing of Stroud, publishers of local history books in the 'Britain in Old Photographs' series, sought our help with their proposed Black Country coverage. Over the next 10 years some 80 Black Country titles were published, many by members of the Black Country Society, with total sales of in excess of 120,000. Every book carries a page about the Black Country Society which has also benefited by selling the books. The series has put more than 16,000 old photographs of the Black Country into the public domain.

In Section 3 are some of my other contributions to the magazine, including my first article, 'Working on the Railway, at 12 Years of Age' and I have included in Section 4 some of my reviews of important books about the Black Country.

Section 5 contains the last collection of my Black Country jokes, supplemented by cartoons by the late Len Pardoe to whom I supplied the captions. Another 300 Black Country jokes were included in my *More Black Country Humour, Tales and Verse,* (1994, 1997, 2001 and 2007), and 100 more in *Stan Hill's Brierley Hill and Life* (published 2002).

Stan Hill, Wordsley, 2009.

# 1.
# Defending and promoting The Black Country

**EDITORIAL**   Winter 1988

I record my sincere thanks to old and new contributors, old and new advertisers, friends and former colleagues, for their support and encouragement in my editing this magazine.

There are now some 25,000 additional back issues of 'The Blackcountryman' in circulation in the area following the Committee's decision a year ago to off-load them from stock. This availability has encouraged some 250 people to take out subscriptions. With new members' sudden acquisition of about 6,000 pages of local material, a means of searching for specific items is required. This is where 'Conspectus Vols. 1 - 20' comes in useful. In this issue's 'Pull Out' will be found 'Conspectus Addendum Vol. 21' to bring the summary up to date. An additional aid 'Thematic Conspectus Vols. 1 - 20' is being printed and will soon be available. This is a compilation of titles and whereabouts of magazine articles over the past 20 years on particular themes, e.g. Coal, Iron and Steel, Canals, Railways, Churches, Chapels, Inns, Motor Cars and Motor Cycles, Trams and Trolley Buses, Dialect and 20 different townships, etc. Thus if you wish to read up about Black Country railways, turn up the appropriate section and there is a list of 52 articles and details of in which issue each appear.

1

# EDITORIAL    Autumn 1988

MUCH of my last year's summer holiday was spent working through the first 20 volumes of 'The Blackcountryman' preparing a summary of the contents for schools' use and now also available to members in booklet form: 'Conspectus: Vols. 1 - 20'. The task took far longer than anticipated because I lingered over each issue reading articles which I had missed, deferred or forgotten after the first time round, always intending to go back to the magazine after the initial perusal but never actually doing so. On completion of the task, after scanning some 5,000 pages and reading or re-reading many of the 800 articles and 160 book reviews therein, my long held admiration for the work of Harold Parsons, as Editor, was reinforced.

Judging by the letters received following Harold's retirement as Editor, this high regard for his work with the magazine is generally held. The letter on page 64 from J. T. Whitehouse is representative of many. John Fletcher recalls the beginnings on page 8.

I am most grateful to Harold for his help in preparing this issue and to Mrs. Parsons for guidance about the advertisers. It is reassuring to know that they can be called upon for advice in the future. The Society is fortunate too in having such an experienced Editor still available for work on future publications.

The Conspectus should help members to find articles more easily than indiscriminate searching, but what is really needed is an index. Perhaps some local Further Educaton establishment may sometime employ a research fellow and computer operator for the task. I can think of less valuable topics which have occupied researchers in the past!

I am encouraged by the offers of articles. Do please continue to send them in and also suggestions for future developments.

Please make good use of the 'Pull Out' both for ordering publications and recruiting new members. Any leads for new advertisers would also be welcome. For the Society and magazine to develop, more members and advertisers are needed.

# EDITORIAL   Summer 1991

Put the children to bed, turn off the television set and settle down to spend a couple of enthralling hours with 'The Blackcountryman'. There are more scoops in this issue: page 12, an interview with Sir Jack Hayward; page 31, an exclusive article by Richard Bond giving details about the Prime Minister's Black Country forebears, and incidently a lesson in tracing one's ancestors; Dr. Rex Bayliss contributes an account of the Somers involved with Messrs. Walter Somers of Halesowen, page 38, and our regular writer, John Sparry, himself a percussionist, reports on his interview with totally deaf percussion virtuoso, Evelyn Glennie – see page 16.

Welcome to canal enthusiasts who make their way to the National Canal Boat Rally at Bumblehole in August. There are several canal articles to interest them particularly: see pages, 19, 27, 45 and 69.

In the remaining articles are reminiscences, a railway article, humour, poetry, reviews, letters, and more.

This is the 12th magazine which I have edited since taking over in September 1988.

During the nine months between my appointment and assuming the editorial chair, when I was charged with disposing of some 40,000 back issues, which I was able to do with the consent on my then gaffer, Ron Westerby, Dudley's Chief Education Officer, I was able to lay the foundations of my editorship. The sale of several hundred complete sets of 'The Blackcountryman' to schools, and their recruitment to Black Country Society membership provided a basis for expansion. Schools' investment in the Society's publications will prove invaluable to them in connection with the 'Local History' element of the new National Curriculum in History. Of the scores of friends and colleagues whom I asked to consider writing for the magazine, after 12 issues, more than 60 have had their contributions included.

I would like to thank all contributors, of long standing and new ones, old and new advertisers. Society Officials and Committee and over 40 new sales persons for their help and encouragement. Last but not least, special thanks to my distinguished predecessor, Harold Parsons, whom I see regularly and whose encouragement, advice and quiet approval I have found most supportive.

We are now in a good position to prepare to launch a number of events in 1992 to celebrate 25 years of existence of the Black Country Society. An outline of what is proposed will be found in the Secretary's Report on page 9. I appeal to members to play a part in the 1992 celebrations and thus help to widen the scope and influence of the Society. There will be a wide variety of items arranged and an opportunity for everyone to contribute in some way or other.

For each issue of the magazine I prepare a synopsis (conspectus!) of the contents for the media. Very occasionally one of the dozen or so recipients uses something for this hand-out with a brief reference in their publication. It puzzles me that nobody has yet paid the slightest attention to any of my scoops, eg the article by an American millionaire about Fred Carder, the revealing profiles of Julie Walters, Sue Lawley, Lord Tombs, Chairman of Rolls-Royce, the article about a Quarry Bank lady, once a circus artiste in Australia. Still – local newspapers are not what they were. Local historians of the future will not glean from the 1990s local newspapers the comprehensive details of life that are available to us from the local press of the 1920 – 1970 period. This is where 'The Blackcountryman' and journals like it must serve to fill the gap.

Is Mr. William Davies, Chairman of the English Tourist Board, with his unacceptable suggestion that the term 'Black Country' be dropped from the description of our sub-region trying to join the ranks of those faceless bureaucrats who, in the 1974 local government re-organisation erased 1,000 years of history in favour of the anonymity of such names as Kirkless and Calderdale? Dudley is lucky still to be Dudley. We might have become 'Dudhalesbrierbridge'. Three cheers for staunch Black Country man, Sir Michael Higgs, who, as Chairman of Worcestershire County Council fought off the re-organisers and insisted that the names of the ancient cathedral cities be retained in the name of the new county, Hereford-Worcester, instead of Malvershire, Severnside, Elgar County (sounds like Texas!).

But how could something which doesn't exist officially be dropped? You will not find the term 'Black Country' on maps. It is in the minds of the people born here, and has been for over 100 years. Go home Mr. Davies and leave the promotion of the Black Country to those Black Country folk born here or by adoption, with a real commitment to the place.

There's plenty of good reading here. (As my old granny used to say about a well-known Sunday newspaper).

Thank you for buying this magazine, whether by subscription or from a shop. I hope that you enjoy parts of it at least, and if you have, buy the next issue as well and encourage your friends to do so too, or better still, take out subscriptions.

Have a good holiday.

3

# EDITORIAL   Spring 1992

THIS year's Black Country Society 25th Anniversary gives us a good opportunity to widen our appeal and increase membership. Plans for a variety of celebratory events are well advanced and support from members and organisations has exceeded expectations. Details of the events will be found in this issue. If you feel that you could contribute do please contact a committee member.

We hope that members living away from the Black Country will be able to return to their roots for the Local History Fair. Details of accommodation available, from the most modest to the most luxurious, is listed in a leaflet available from the Director of Black Country Tourism, Priory Hall, Dudley, DY1 4EU, for a second class stamp. The Society will produce a leaflet of easily accessible evening events in early April for those who might be able to make this return.

As Editor I get very little feedback about the contents of the magazine and when there are comments they are usually contradictory. For example, in January I had a complaint that Walsall never received a mention, and the letter on page 76 " . . . . . why is it always about Walsall . . . . ?". Attention is given to trying to achieve a balance over a period. In this issue the following townships are represented in articles: Brierley Hill, Coseley, Darlaston, Dudley, Halesowen, Kingswinford, Oldbury, Sandwell, Sedgley, Smethwick, Tipton, Walsall, Wednesbury, Wolverhampton and the Wyre Forest.

This quarter's Black Country personality is a remarkable lady who is remembered by many who have had associations with Wordsley Hospital. Details of her training will amaze younger readers educated at universities and colleges during the past 30 years.

Michael Hale contributes an article to remind us of what the Black Country was like only a few years ago and attributes its industrial decline to interfering governments. John Sparry has unearthed the story of a 24 year old Kingswinford lad killed in a raid on Nuremberg in 1944. He had completed his quota of operations and should have been resting but because of heavy losses of aircrew volunteered for additional duties. The account is a tribute to Fl. Lieut. Bob Cadman, D.F.M. and to those who made the supreme sacrifice.

Two Society members whose researches into the history of the Black Country's water supplies have opened my eyes to the contribution that this service has made to the elimination of disease during the past 150 years write about the supply of safe water to Dudley and give the background to a well-known landmark.

Three newcomers to these pages contribute articles. Anne Harvey 'discovered' Noel Brettell after I did and tells why and how. Monica Homer writes about her father, a good Black Country man and John C. Popple gives the background about the main feature on one of our summer walks. Walsall folk can learn why there is a Darwall Street in that town and Tipton folk will discover details of a local dynasty but not of the name given in the title of that article. To complete this quarter's fare read about Wolverhampton's last commercial cinema, and a new one there, why Sandwell is more interesting than you thought, a one time Smethwick industry, the 'best buys' in books you'll get this year, and much more.

I hope that all readers will find something of interest.

Last year I wrote to Sir Bob Reid, Chairman of British Rail, to suggest to him that a British Rail locomotive should be named 'The Blackcountryman' and enclosed reasons to support the idea. The suggestion was not dismissed out of hand but passed onto the Midland Region for consideration. Since then support has come from The Black Country Director of Tourism, Dudley Chamber of Industry and Commerce and the Black Country Development Corporation. If you are a member of a local body which likes the idea, get a resolution of support passed and send it to Sir Bob Reid, Post Office Box 100, London, NW1 1DZ.

See you at the celebrations.

4

# EDITORIAL  Summer 1992

IT is with regret that we report the death on 7th May 1992 of Harold Parsons, the first Editor of 'The Blackcountryman', who had been in poor health for some years. In a 'Tribute' on page 10, Jack Haden outlines Harold's great contribution to the Black Country Society and gives details of some of his writing successes.

Since succeeding Harold as Editor in 1988 I saw him regularly when he was, as ever, forthright in his comments, generous with his praise, and always helpful. He continued to write for this magazine until just before his death. This issue includes two of his items and in April he completed an important item for the October issue. We record our deepest sympathy to Joan his wife, business associate and nurse.

It was pleasing to make contact at the 25th Anniversary Local History Fair with so many members whom we do not see at evening meetings. The Fair and associated events attracted considerable publicity and we are particularly grateful to the *Express & Star* for the advertising feature and their coverage. For those unable to attend, there is a report of the events on page 53. The celebratory activities continue. The Walks Programme has started well with attendances of 91, 103 and 62 and there have been enjoyable excursions to Ashorne Hall, Lichfield and the Wedgwood Museum and a Sunday afternoon walk in the Sandwell Valley. There is more to come.

In the Black Country Personalities series I am pleased to be able to record the achievements for the Black Country of Don and Roy Richardson. They have brought to the Black Country 21st Century developments. Dudley's centre of gravity has moved to Merry Hill. How convenient it would be if the whole of Dudley's local government administration moved to The Waterfront leaving Dudley centre to be redeveloped for tourism, residents and leisure.

Many readers will remember the Wednesbury bakery of Hickinbottom and Sons Ltd. Mr. Geoffrey Hickinbottom has kindly supplied all the information for the article on the beginnings, growth and disappearance of a huge Black Country firm. Monica Homer recalls how her parents befriended two German POWs in 1946 and reports the recent reminiscences of one of them. Joan R. Rawlings of Kent sportingly responded to my challenge to write something after she had complained that there was never anything in the magazine about Langley and Causeway Green – well now there is!

Keith Cheetham, ever active in promoting Black Country tourism, describes how he rose to the challenge in the USA, further evidence that he 'never misses an opportunity; and the Dean of Guernsey tells of his friendship with Black Country born Zimbabwean poet Noel H. Brettell who died in December 1991.

There are articles by regular contributors C. J. L. Elwell, Ted Jukes, John Sparry, Michael Hale, Ron Davies who has the centre pages as well, and Bill Pace, and old friends Arthur Truby and H. L. Kershaw return with interesting pieces. If you have 'Bats in the Belfrey' read Ray Weston on page 39.

The October issue of 'The Blackcountryman' will be the 100th and we hope to make it a special. Do please publicise the magazine amongst your friends and encourage them to subscribe. Membership continues to grow – can we have a big effort to reach 2,000 before the end of this 25th Anniversary Year?

Have a good holiday. Take the magazine with you if you haven't finished it before departing.

# EDITORIAL    Autumn 1992

1992 has been a memorable year for the Black Country Society. We have worked our way through an extensive programme of 25th Anniversary celebratory events. This 100 page 'special' issue of the 100th 'The Blackcountryman' is the penultimate item, the final one to be the Dudley Schools Writing Competition (with a Black Country theme, of course), the prizes for which are funded by the Francis Brett Young Society.

We have disposed of the Chairman of the English Tourist Board's suggestion that the term 'Black Country' be dropped and 'put down' vigorously one or two individuals who made ill-informed criticism of the Society in the press (" . . . so-called Black Country Society" – indeed!)

The National Federation of Retail Newsagents is promoting 'The Blackcountryman' in more than 50 shops in the Walsall and Wolverhampton areas and the Society is being represented by speakers and sales stalls all over the Black Country and beyond.

The Membership Secretary recently reported that membership had reached 1,975; a big effort by existing members before Christmas and we should reach our target of 2,000 in 1992.

We wish to record our sincere thanks to all who have contributed to the Society's 25th Anniversary Programme which we hope has increased the public's awareness of the existence of the Black Country Society and 'The Blackcountryman'.

It is appropriate that this issue includes a history of the first 25 years of the Society. I first asked Harold Parsons to write this nearly two years ago, a task he willingly undertook. As he had edited the first 83 issues of 'The Blackcountryman' and took a close interest in the affairs of the Society right up to his death, he was perfectly placed to do it. He had finished the article just before he went into hospital for the last time.

'Never miss an opportunity', said King George V to the Prince of Wales in preparation for kingship. With this in mind I thought I'd tell an artist whose exhibition I had chanced upon when on a speaking engagement at the Stone Manor Hotel last year, about 'our mon at the Royal Academy' (See Vol. 24 No. 4). My letter, unlike so many of my appeals which get binned, brought a response which has led to a fruitful association for the Society. The artist, Nigel Hallard, FRSA, is this issue's Black Country Personality.

Seven new contributors join ranks with a dozen or so regulars in this 'special' issue in which I hope that all readers will find items to interest them. It is pleasing to have plenty of material from which to try to achieve a balance between subject, area and period and I hope that contributors who have not yet seen their work in print will be patient. There are too many items for individual comments but I do commend to you a new contributor's poem 'The Deserted Nest at Wordsley' (page 71), a sad story sensitively expressed.

The Black Country Society enters its 26th year stronger than ever with this magazine which keeps us all in contact. We are grateful to all who play a part: contributors, distributors, advertisers and unofficial publicists. There must be a special thanks to Martyn Round, Managing Director of Reliance Printing Works and Society member, who takes a personal interest in the magazine's production and to whom nothing is too much trouble in order to translate my requirements into the finished product on the due date. (See Martyn's letter on page 98).

Do please 'spread the word' so that this time next year we can report continued progress.

Happy Christmas and I promise at least one amazing story hitherto untold, amongst plenty of 'good reading' in the January 1993 issue.

6

# EDITORIAL    Winter 1993

The 100th issue of 'The Blackcountryman' was well received and despite an extra 750 being printed we were searching for copies by the end of October to satisfy orders. Some of these will have to wait until we take back unsold copies from our stockists. Casual readers are urged to take out a subscription (see the Pull-Out) to ensure receiving each issue and other benefits of Black Country Society membership.

An amazing story was promised for this issue. Turn to, page 10 and read about Ken Downing. I hope that readers will find plenty to interest them amongst the other dozen or so contributions.

Attention is drawn to the book review on page 82. "Britain Since 1930" ('Timespan' series) is by Society member Dr. John West and is interesting to members in that he has included in a 32 page section entitled 'Ordinary Folk', 12 articles from past issues of 'The Blackcountryman'. This book and others in the series publicise the Society and magazine throughout the country.

A second satellite branch of the Black Country Society is now firmly established at Kingswinford and a full programme has been arranged for 1993 (see page 9). The Wyre Forest branch continues to thrive with a wide variety of informative and recreational activities. An invitation is extended to all members to attend any of the branch meetings on a casual or regular basis for any event which interests them.

Best wishes for 1993.

# EDITORIAL    Summer 1994

IF readers in reading this magazine get a fraction of the enjoyment which I derive in compiling it, they will have their money's worth. In five years as Editor I have met many interesting, exciting, unusual, eccentric (by their own admission) people, not all of whose stories have yet been told in these pages. In fact, meeting them has given me another lecture title, 'Some Black Country Characters' which has been well received by two audiences so far. From this issue I can add two more subjects to my list. Designer/Builder George Wood's philosophy and work are remarkable. Although I have known Jim Mason for over 40 years it is only recently that I have uncovered his most interesting life story. Those who believe that there are no 'characters' in the Black Country now must be troglodytes.

We have achieved the 1992 target of 2,000 members but it will need continuous effort to keep that figure and improve upon it. Please spread the word whenever you have the opportunity and enrol new members if you can. Have you a contact who could order copies of 'The Blackcountryman' to give clients (one member does this already) or staff? About 10 subscriptions are taken out each year as presents for friends and relations – could we increase this number? Do you know anyone who would advertise herein? Advertising revenue for this issue is a record. We need to keep the adverts coming in order to keep the cover price steady – there has been no increase since 1988. Is this a record for a magazine? A 'selling factor' is that we are non-commercial and that nobody receives payment for their contributions. Please do what you can to help.

Book Saturday September 17th 1994 (yes next year!) for another huge Black Country Society event which will have great appeal. Details will emerge. Have a good holiday.

# EDITORIAL Winter 1994

HAPPY New Year to all Black Country Society members and casual readers. To the latter group we extend an invitation to join us as members in what promises to be an exciting year for the Society. There are considerable benefits to be gained from being a member of the Black Country Society. There are three meeting venues at which monthly meetings are held (see page 9) and may soon be a fourth, a Summer 'Walks in the Black Country and its Green Borderland' programme, bargain remaindered books, our own publications, a Victorian style concert party and holidays organised by the Wyre Forest Branch, contacts with other folk interested in and proud of their Black Country heritage, and 'The Blackcountryman' delivered each quarter to keep us all in touch.

There is a suggestion that we stage a lunchtime meeting, quarterly or bi-monthly and we have a volunteer to organise this. The meeting place could be at Savacentre, Oldbury, where lunch in the cafeteria, or a buffet, could be taken followed by a speaker or entertainment in the functions room there, and an opportunity for members to meet. This may appeal to some who do not like going out at night and Oldbury is well served by 'buses. Anyone interested is invited to inform the Editor and if there is sufficient response a date will be set in late April for the first meeting.

We are now working towards the Black Country Society Day at the Black Country Museum on Saturday 17th September 1994 when there will be a massive get-together of members and friends. Sufficient sponsorship money has already been raised to ensure an excellent Society programme being held there on that day in addition to the 30 or so regular attractions at this fine award winning open air museum. Already one member from Brighton has sent his ticket money and several overseas members have written to say that they will attend. Further details will be given in the Easter issue of this magazine but in the meantime enter the date in your new diaries and don't let anything supersede it.

In this issue two articles particularly draw attention to Black Country folks' craftsmanship. Charles Elwell retraces Burritt's journey which Hobbes followed too. Both of these 19th Century Black Country explorers were noting those fields where Black Country innovations and expertise led the world. Nearer to the present, W. L. Downes writes about the ingenuity of Black Country craftsmen in chainmaking. Our Black Country Personality this quarter is internationally known Harry Eccleston O.B.E., whose artistic work you have all carried about in your wallets and purses. He believes that the background of craftsmanship in his growing up, the superb engineers of his boyhood, the builders of the record breaking Sunbeam and the like, and that pride in craftsmanship, set him a most valuable pattern for his future life.

There are pieces by four new contributors, the usual pages of reviews, letters and humour, with writers well known to readers completing a magazine in which I hope that all who peruse its pages will find something of interest.

8

# EDITORIAL    Winter 1995

THE Black Country Society made considerable progress in 1994 with regular meetings at 4 venues, an extensive programme of Summer walks and excursions, the Society's Day at the Black Country Museum, our association with Messrs. Alan Sutton Publishing Ltd. with the launch of Ian Bott's 'Wednesbury in Old Photographs', the first in their Black Country series, associating with the Express & Star with the publication of Society member Gladys Welsh's 'A Curate's Egg' and a new book of our own which is selling well. We have had much press coverage and this together with talks to clubs, societies and schools, and having sales stalls at functions, has led to the steady recruitment of new members.

As only about 10% of our membership can attend meetings the Society 'flagship' is, of course, this magazine. This is the link for members worldwide and our thanks are due to all who contribute to its production.

In this issue, our Black Country Personality, Len Pardoe, recalls the day when half of Quarry Bank might have been wiped out and Dr. John Fletcher writes about another terrifying wartime episode experienced by a Black Country man. Charles Elwell tells us how electricity came to the Black Country and Ray Bowling and Mary Bodfish deal with aspects of 19th century Halesowen and Smethwick. Dr. Kenneth Russell's Summer issue article on the 1954 Brierley Hill gypsies prompted from the U.S.A. a letter recalling the writer's involvement with the tribe. There are contributions from a dozen more members and from the score of items in this issue I hope that all readers will find something of interest.

Happy New Year.

\* \* \* \*

# SOCIETY NEWS

JACK Purcell has relinquished the post of stock controller and postal sales officer after 5 years. Our thanks are due to him for this valuable work for the Society. The duties will be shared by Society Vice President Malcolm Lacey who has taken charge of the stock room and Alan Pilkington who will deal with postal sales. (see page 80).

*Details of the 1995 Programme of Black Country Walks and Excursions will be distributed with the Spring issue of 'The Blackcountryman'.*

During 1994 the Editor addressed 24 groups about the Society.

*The 1994 Carol Concert at Mount Tabor Methodist Church, Woodsetton was attended by the Mayors of Dudley, Walsall and Wolverhampton and the Deputy Mayor of Sandwell.*

An extra 300 Autumn magazines were printed (3,300) for Museum Day on 17th September but only 40 were sold there. However our usual outlets have done very well with this issue and all the extra magazines have been distributed.

*Launched on 17th September at the Museum the Society's 'More Black Country Humour, Tales & Verse' has done well. In the first 10 weeks over 500 were sold. The Committee is considering two more titles for publication in 1995.*

Since its foundation 5 years ago the Society's Wyre Forest Branch's concert party 'Cum Sing Wi' We' has helped to raise over £14,000 for charity.

*We are pleased to be associated with The Express & Star in the publication of 'The Curate's Egg', the memoirs of 85 year old Society member Gladys M. Welsh. In the first week of publication over 1,000 copies were sold throughout the Black Country.*

9

# EDITORIAL   Spring 1997

THIS issue is without Past President Ron Davies's planned contribution as in early April he sustained a nasty broken leg and was in hospital for a time. This prevented him from completing his fieldwork so that item will appear next year. We all wish Ron a speedy return to the Society scene.

Several new writers' articles are included in this magazine. These include an account about a one time Principal of Dudley Art School, Ivo Shaw, by his son Robin, reminiscences of a Wednesbury childhood by Margaret Perry, and Peter Skidmore's account about the Dudley election of 1874.

It is surprising how many readers mention that on receiving the magazine they turn first to the Black Country Humour page. A Clebak cartoon is included on page 65 to illustrate a 'glass' joke based on a true story. Read this and then look closely at the object blown by the glassblower.

Our publication "More Black Country Humour, Tales & Verse" has proved to be our best seller for several years with over 1,600 sold in 8 months since the launch at the Museum on 17th September last. After two recent talks when I quoted some of the jokes, read 5 poems and one of the stories from the book I sold 65 and 26 copies respectively. We have another title in the pipeline for publication in the Autumn. This too should be a best seller.

There are so many notices this quarter about books produced by members that there is no room for detailed reviews. Jim Boulton's new 'Black Country Road Vehicles' will be launched in July. This is in the series with which the Society is associated with Alan Sutton Publishing Ltd.

Have a good Summer holiday. In the Autumn we shall have more interesting reading and wide ranging programmes of meetings at four venues for you to enjoy.

# EDITORIAL    Autumn 1995

THIS issue's Black Country Personality, Bill Swaithes, was on the Brierley Hill scene 20 years before me so we had much to discuss when I called on him to talk about his life.

There are articles by several new contributors, including John Wilkes, an enthusiastic Staffordshire Bull Terrier owner who gives the breed's background in this 60th year of recognition as a pedigree dog by the Kennel Club, and Dianne Mannering records how Dudley Castle was gambled away by 'Lord Quodon' ('former'), but there's more of that story to come. Peggy Childs tells how day nurseries came into existence during the war and developed into an important part of education provision, and Margaret Pearce recalls the contribution made by Woodside Military Band to the social life of the district. Dr. H. Max White's account about his father's pharmacy business will stir older readers' memories about health care between the wars.

I am grateful to regular contributors whose meticulous research into their subjects results in absorbing articles. At the other end of the spectrum, Black Country Humour is now 2 pages. Where do the jokes come from? Members, mainly. We shall soon have enough for another compilation. Keep them coming.

Amongst the interesting 'phone calls received lately was one from an 88 year old at Hull and former pupil at Ivo Shaw's Dudley Art School, who told me about his career as an engraver, and in connection with an article in preparation, Sir Stanley Matthews, C.B.E., spent 10 minutes recalling his memories of a former England team-mate. Never a dull moment!

11

# EDITORIAL   Spring 1996

ON 31st January H.R.H. The Prince of Wales visited the Black Country. At the Waterfront Business and Commercial Park which straddles the Dudley No. 1. Canal, next to the gigantic Merry Hill Shopping Centre, and where 5% of the nation's steel requirement was once produced, he met Society Life Members Messrs. Don and Roy Richardson, the developers. The Prince commented favourably on what he saw so I sent him a copy of 'The Blackcountryman' in which the brothers are featured, and also the current issue, together with my 'Brierley Hill in Old Photographs' so that he could compare images of the past with what he had seen.

The Prince's Assistant Private Secretary wrote that the Prince was most interested to peruse all of the publications and offered congratulations on their production. He had greatly enjoyed his visit and received something of a feel for the heritage of the area and he asked that his very best wishes be passed on to members of the Black Country Society.

By a coincidence, this issue's Black Country Personality (No. 31) once held the post of Assistant Private Secretary to the Prince of Wales. Black Country Man David John Wright's progress in the Diplomatic Service to the important position of Her Majesty's Ambassador to Japan is recorded on pages 10 to 12.

This issue's 'menu' includes a touching account by Vera Dando of a visit to her grandfather's First World War grave in France which reminds us of the suffering experienced by millions in two world wars. Dr. John West gives some clues about a well-known Headmaster and appeals to older Old Hill and Cradley Heath folk, and anyone else interested, to turn detective and pursue them. There is an account about the very profitable association between the Society and Messrs. Alan Sutton Publishing Ltd., producers of the 'Britain (and now 'Black Country') in Old Photographs' series. Peter Skidmore's analysis of an 1857 election poster shows that present day elections are tame affairs compared with those of 140 years ago.

It is pleasing to note that there are 5 new contributors in this issue and that our well established writers continue to serve us well. Don't give up when you get to page 74, there are some interesting book reviews and letters.

We are in for an interesting year: more books to be published, Society attendances at exhibitions, our Local History Fair, the extended Summer Walks Programme, interesting programmes at 4 venues and of course two more issues of 'The Blackcountryman' which has recently had very favourable mentions in two national history journals.

* * * *

## MEMBERSHIP

On 23rd February 1996 there were 2,204 paid-up members of the Black Country Society.

* * * *

12

# EDITORIAL   Autumn 1996

1996, so far, has been the busiest time ever for the Black Country Society with a new group at Kidderminster – there are now 5 venues, see page 7 – an extended Summer Walks and Excursions programme, a two day Local History Fair, two book launches, talks to other groups, sales stalls at local events and local radio interviews. The resulting press publicity has been the best we have ever had followed by a steady flow of new members. It was a relief to be able to sit down for a few hours in August to concentrate on assembling this issue.

Our Black Country Personality is young man tipped by music critics to make a name for himself. Stefan Asbury's Black Country education, and particularly Dudley Education Department's Music Services (instrument tuition) set him on the road to an unusual career. Our late Past-President, Keith Gale, is remembered with a most interesting account, updated, of how a small Black Country manufacturing company has moved with the times to survive. There are two new contributors and we are grateful to them and to our established writers, the quality of whose work is widely recognised in local history circles.

On 18 afternoons over a period of six weeks, Society members manned the Merry Hill Tourist Information Centre to register overseas visitors in Black Country Tourism's 'Welcome Home' programme and some interesting contacts were made.

In 1997 we shall mark the Black Country Society's 30 years existence with celebratory events which we hope will appeal to members. In the meantime the most extensive Autumn programme ever offered should encourage more members to come and make contact, even if only occasionally.

13

# EDITORIAL    Spring 1997

THE position of the regular feature 'Black Country Personalities' has been moved to pages 37 to 41, better to accommodate photographs kindly loaned by the subject, last year's Lord Mayor of London, Tipton born Sir John Chalstrey. The brief account of this most distinguished Black Country man's career, achievements and Lord Mayoral record will amaze readers.

Detective work by our President which has solved a question which has long puzzled industrial historians about how S.S. Titanic's anchor was transported from Noah Hingley's to the railway, is recorded in his article. This is published while the Dudley Art Gallery magnificent Titanic Exhibition is still on as it has been extended until September 14th.

The Humour section has been extended to 3 pages as Whitbread Novel Award winner Beryl Bainbridge has sportingly given her permission for a 'tongue-in-cheek' article she wrote for a national newspaper to be included so that I can 'have a go at her'. Coincidently, Ms Bainbridge's award winning novel, *Everyman for Himself* is the story of the Titanic disaster of April 1912 as seen through the eyes of Morgan the nephew of the shipping line owner.

The dialect narrative poem The Pitman's Dissent published in 1883 by Tom Brown (our past-President? – if it's him, 'e ay arf wearin' well!) is worth reading carefully. Note the non-conformist bias.

Thanks to our 3 new contributors and our regular writers whose efforts help to bring you a magazine which I hope you will find interesting.

14

# EDITORIAL Autumn 1997

THE Black Country Society's Association with Sutton Publishing Limited, publishers of the 'Britain in Old Photographs' series, has continued to our advantage. With eight Black Country books in the series and five more to be launched before the end of the year, each with the Society's advertising panel and logo on more than 20,000 books altogether, we have never before had such widespread publicity. The Society has also had good newspaper coverage and mentions on local radio and television. In addition many members 'fly the flag' with Society stalls at events, talks to other societies and as our representatives on various Black Country committees.

Not much seems to be known locally about John Northwood I's sons who emigrated to the United States of America. Harry and Carl Northwood became prominent for over 30 years from 1880 in the American glass tableware industry. Dr. James S. Measell has kindly contributed an article which will help to fill the gap. On this subject, there is a rare opportunity to view the amazing Notley-Lerpiniere collection of carnival glass (over 700 pieces), including 74 Northwood pieces at Broadfield House Glass Museum, Kingswinford. The exhibition will close on 19th October.

On the 100th anniversary of Queen Victoria's Diamond Jubilee, much attention is being paid to the Victorian Age. The Black Country's contribution to the Raj is being researched by Peter J. English and we are privileged to be able to include details of his findings relating to Black Country firms' work in the Indian subcontinent. In this issue he chronicles some of the achievements of Messrs. Braithwaite and Kirk of West Bromwich.

# EDITORIAL    Winter 1997

DURING the Autumn three more Black Country titles have been launched in Sutton Publishing Ltd.'s *Britain in Old Photographs* series bringing the total to 11. In these books some 2,500 photographs of the Black Country have been made available to a wide public and 25,000 books printed, each carrying the Black Country Society information panel and logo.

On 10th October David Vodden's *Walsall in Old Photographs* was launched by the Mayor of Walsall, Cllr. Norman Matthews and on the next morning at Lye Community Centre Pat Dunn's *Lye and Wollescote in Old Photographs* was launched by Len Pardoe (Black Country Personality No. 26 in Vol. 28 No. 1 of *The Blackcountryman*). Pat, who is Programme Secretary of the Society's Phoenix (Kidderminster) branch had been working on the book for two years with Denys Brooks when he died suddenly early this year. With the help of the Coroner and Denys's nephew the material was retrieved from Denys's house and Pat was able to complete the preparations. Over 100 people attended the launch for a most successful sales and social occasion.

The third launch was in the Amblecote Room of the Stourbridge Town Hall complex on 31st October for Bob Clarke's and Michael Reuter's *Stourbridge, Wollaston and Amblecote in Old Photographs* when the special guest was Debra Shipley, Member of Parliament for Stourbridge. The Chairman invited Ms Shipley to consider herself a Black Country person under his definition, "The Black Country is a State of Mind" she immediately established her credentials with the information that both her parents, from West Bromwich and Smethwick, are Black Country folk. As an author herself, she congratulated the compilers of the book and Sutton Publishing Ltd. for helping to cement Black Country townships' civic pride with this series of books and the Black Country Society for their enthusiastic response to the Publisher's approach in 1994.

Two more titles will be released before the end of 1997: *Sedgley and District – A Second Selection* – and *Tipton – A Second Selection*, and several more are planned for 1998.

These new books which have a slightly larger format than the first six in the series may be obtained from bookshops at £9.99p each. Society members may obtain them from the Postal Sales Officer at the cover price which will include postage.

Ron Julian, Membership Secretary, reported at the last Committee meeting that the society now has 2,462 members, the highest ever recorded, can you enrol another member so that we can reach 2,500 by the A.G.M.?

In this issue articles cover 15 Black Country townships from Bilston to Brierley Hill and Wolverhampton to West Bromwich. We welcome two new contributors, thank all our regulars for their continued support, and in this Christmas season extend to all readers, advertisers and all who have helped the Black Country Society in 1997, the Compliments of the Season.

16

# EDITORIAL    Summer 1998

A COUPLE of months ago a *Birmingham Post* reporter rang to tell me that a discussion paper from a Sandwell Corporation seminar to the appropriate committee included a suggestion that the term '**The Black Country**' might be dropped and 'The Grey Country' substituted to reflect its changing environment and economy.

I checked that it wasn't April 1st and gave as a brief response, "I don't believe it. The suggestion is barmy!'

The term '**The Black Country**' was originally coined in the 1850s and used by various writers, the best known of that period, probably, Elihu Burritt for his book *Walks in the Black Country and its Green Borderland* (Sampson Low, Son, and Marston, 1868). It is only in the past 25 years that the term has really had some official recognition, Sandwell Corporation itself contributing to this with its acceptance as being a **Black Country** Metropolitan Borough.

The **Black Country** Society, one of the largest sub-regional societies in the country with some 2,500 members, has been campaigning for 31 years for wider recognition of the term **The Black Country**. In the Dudley telephone directory there are now 57 firms listed with the prefix **Black Country**, and 56 in the Wolverhampton directory. Twelve years ago the **Black Country** Development Corporation was established by the Government and 11 years ago **Black Country** Tourism was set up by the four **Black Country** boroughs. The **Black Country** Living Museum attracts about a quarter of a million visitors annually and there is now a **Black Country** History Consortium representing local history societies in the four **Black Country** boroughs.

Has the Sandwell seminar suggestion proposer any knowledge of **Black Country** history?

As studies of the Victorian period have intensified in recent years the greatness of the area known as the **Black Country**, for its inventiveness, ingenuity and hard work has become more recognised and residents, and pupils as a result of the National Curriculum, have become proud of their heritage which the long established term, **The Black Country**, implies, represents and encapsulates.

It is particularly inappropriate that the unacceptable suggestion comes from Sandwell for from that area came much of the industrial enterprise which put the 'Great' into 'Great Britain' in Victorian and Edwardian times via such well-known firms as Braithwaite & Kirk, Patent Shaft & Axeltree Company, Horseley Iron Company, Albright & Wilson, Accles & Pollock, Babcock & Wilcox, Barrows & Hall, Salter's, Kenrick's, Hudson's, Chance Brothers, B.I.P. Only a non-**Black Country** person would make such an inapt suggestion at that seminar. Perhaps **Black Country** Borough Councils should hold '**Black Country** Background Familiarisation' days for those new employees imported from south of the Watford Gap to administer us.

After taking a pasting from television and the local press about the apparent suggestion Sandwell's 'Regeneration Chair' (Aynuk says: "Wos one o' them?) issued a press release which stated: *All that's happened is that we went through an exercise looking at the future of Sandwell considering a number of scenarios. We had to consider a number of differing factors, particularly looking at the economy and the environment. We obviously will be trying to drive forward a successful economy with an improving environment but it is important as an exercise that we look at all the possible outcomes. In no way did we intend that the name should change . . . . . . .*

Good, but let's hope that documents which come into the public domain state exactly what they mean in future and 'foreign' officials should note that we don't want anyone writing out our **Black Country** history.

17

# EDITORIAL   Autumn 1998

IN this issue two important series are concluded: Peter J. English's 'Braithwaite & Kirk' and Charles Elwell's 'The Sanitary Movement in the Black Country'. We have been privileged to have a preview of Peter's on location researches into the tremendous contribution made by Black Country firms to the Raj. His work on the famous West Bromwich company is to be published by Sandwell Community Library Services.

Our Black Country Personality, No. 41 in the series, Professor John Woodhouse has had a remarkable academic career for which the foundations were laid in Quarry Bank. He is now a Society Life Member and has readily agreed to do a bit of work for us in the Autumn. On Friday 13th November at 7 p.m. at Mount Pleasant Primary School, Quarry Bank he will launch Ned Williams's forthcoming book *Quarry Bank in Old Photographs,* accrued from his adult class at that school.

C.J.N. Fletcher has contributed an interesting article about living in the former Oldbury Vicarage as a boy after the Second World War when his father was Vicar of Oldbury. The inhabitants thought that there might be ghosts there and the writer wonders if the spirits were laid to rest when the building was demolished and 13 houses built on the site or whether they still emerge in a sad and fruitless search for their familiar haunting grounds.

This issue marks the start of my 11th year as Editor. Although I have the final responsibility for what is included in the magazine its production is a great team effort. Over the past 10 years there have been over 120 new contributors, there is always a team of willing helpers available to pack 2,000 magazines for posting and hand delivery and to deliver another 1,000 to some 40 sales outlets. Reliance Printers of Halesowen, printers of all 124 magazines over the past 31 years go to endless trouble to convert my 'mock-ups' into an acceptable magazine. Many thanks to all who help, including our Advertisers.

1998 has probably been the busiest ever for the Black Country Society. On pages 5-7 will be found details of Autumn activities, the Local History Fair and book launches. We hope see many members at these events.

Stan Hill.

* * * *

## FAMILY & LOCAL HISTORY FAIR
Saturday/Sunday 26th & 27th September 1998
Dudley Town Hall, 10 a.m. to 4 p.m. Admission Free.
See separate notice for details.

# EDITORIAL   Winter 1998

THIS 125th issue of *The Blackcountryman* marks the start of the 32nd year of its existence making it the oldest regular publication incorporating the term **THE BLACK COUNTRY** in the title.

In December 1995 **Local History Magazine** published its findings of a survey of local history publications and *The Blackcountryman* was listed amongst the best with the comment:

" . . . . . *absolutely crammed full of everything and anything about its area of interest and can leave its readers feeling as if they have feasted on a past made real by the Editor's unstinting enthusiasm for his locality"*.

In the last magazine it was reported that the Society had had a very busy 1998. There has been no respite since September with the Family and Local History Fair, four book launches, the new session's programmes at six venues – the October meetings attracted over 300 members – and several 'Millennium Spectaculars' under consideration.

I am grateful to our contributors who keep me supplied with sufficient articles for the contents page to list a wide range of subjects.

If you are still looking for a Christmas present and cannot think what, do search these pages for details of several Black Country presents on offer: a membership subscription (recipient will also receive an extra free gift), 1999 'Arrowsmith' calendar, one of the recently published 'old photographs' books, or one of those reviewed. Time will be getting short by the time you receive this magazine but every effort will be made to send orders by return of post and thus in time for Christmas.

On behalf of the Committee I would like to wish all readers a Happy Christmas and a Prosperous New Year.

# EDITORIAL   Spring 1999

THERE are three Second World War related items in this issue, two book reviews and an article. The book about Frank Foley who retired to Stourbridge gives some idea of what we in Britain narrowly escaped. Dr. Jack Martin's fascinating article is about British Intelligence and the part played by Walsall born Harry Hinsley in Britain's "holding the fort" until "the New World came to the rescue of the Old". The other review deals with an aspect of the latter. The book concerned demonstrates why the ultimate outcome of the war was inevitable.

I hope that all readers will find something of interest amongst the other dozen or so articles and all the other bits and pieces, ranging from our Black Country Personality to a survey of interesting trees in the area via several industrial items and reminiscences.

The Committee will be reporting at the Annual General Meeting on 24th March on the last financial year and we hope for a good attendance. Last year was very busy and the current year is proving to be even busier with meetings and publications. We look forward to members not involved with the administration of the Society volunteering to help.

# EDITORIAL    Winter 1999

Apologies for the delay in the publication of this issue The Blackcountryman.

The last few months of 1999 must have been the busiest ever for the Black Country Society. There have been book launches for 'Sutton' books, our own 'Sparry' book, others to which Society members have contributed such as Rob Birkbeck's magnificent *A Picture of a Moment in Time* and Sylvia Everitt's/Dianne Mannering's *Staffordshire Millennium Tapestry* which includes Graham Beckley's brilliant photographs, and my own volume; concerts, T.V., radio and newspaper coverage of these events and our second 'sell-out' Arrowsmith calendar with the *Express & Star,* giving the Society more publicity than ever.

It became obvious in November that a special issue of the magazine would not be ready to catch the pre-Christmas post, but here it is at last. I hope that the Spring issue will be posted as usual in March.

In this issue the Black Country Personality No. 46 profile has been moved to the centre pages to accommodate a selection of Black Country artist David Piddock's works. His Nelson's Column painting on the front cover, a reminder of Britain's great past, is an appropriate one to illustrate the first issue of *the Blackcountryman* of the New Millennium. David's story is one of dogged determination in the face of early reverses.

It is sad that the splendid British idea for the 'London Eye', 'the biggest wheel in the world' has so much foreign involvement. The framework was constructed by Dutch engineers, the steel spindle was cast in the Czeck Republic by Skoda, the 32 capsules came from France and include French wooden furniture, the special strong glass came from Italy as did the cables for the wheel's spokes and the capsules' gearboxes were made by a German company. Peter J. English's series of articles about 19th and 20th century Black Country engineering firms' work overseas continues in this issue to remind us that Britain once led the world in constructional and heavy engineering. Thankfully Britain's ingenuity has ensured that the nation continues to earn a good living in the world despite being superseded in some spheres.

Three new Black Country sculptures, all in Dudley Borough as it happens, have been unveiled recently, of Duncan Edwards, John Northwood and one in which the Black Country Society via Ron Moss had an input, namely 'The Legger'. In his account about the unveiling Ron has disclosed a fact which 'turns history on its head' and which I have not seen reported elsehere – see page 62.

Amongst the wide variety of articles is one about Steve Bull, legendary Wolves striker whose record and loyalty to his club have been recognised in the New Year's Honours List and Courtenay V. Smale, a researcher of Ruskin Pottery has contributed a fascinating account about this interesting firm's workforce. And there is plenty more by established and new contributors.

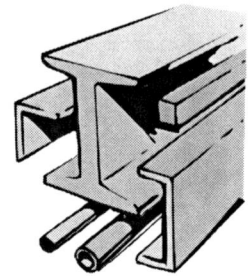

21

# EDITORIAL   Autumn 1999

IN this issue there is a wide spread of articles covering 15 Black Country townships, several general articles and the regular features.

The varied life of Black Country Personality No. 45 – Geoff Hill, will amaze people who have only known him since 1960 or in connection with his fund raising for Mary Stevens' Hospice. For example, at 17 years of age he was British Under 18 Cycling Champion and the business successes he had before finally settling at Amblecote, and his continued success there, confirm that he is a born businessman.

Peter Skidmore's concise analysis of the work of the former Black Country Development Corporation in the 11 years of its existence is worthy of careful study. He records how local pragmatic politicians though opposed in principle to that body, soon participated in its management to make it work for the benefit of the Black Country. The positive results are listed.

Congratulations to Oldbury Repertory Company celebrating 60 years existence this year. Richard Thompson has contributed an interesting account about the history of this leading Black Country amateur theatre which seemed totally professional when I enjoyed a play there earlier this year.

Alf Bradley's *Recollections of a Gravedigger* are amusing and instructive. When he showed Mr. Christopher Firmstone the family tomb several years ago he told him how many of his ancestors had been interred there and added mischievously that there was room for several more.

The beginning of the new millennium is seen by some publishers as a good opportunity for celebratory books. Of all those mentioned in this issue in reviews and advertisements several come into this category. Of particular interest is *Sylvia Everett's Staffordshire Millennium Embroideries* because the Society was instrumental in bringing together the people involved. It was our Secretary's idea to invite Sylvia to exhibit her magnificent creations at last year's Local History Fair where she met Society member/contributor/author Dianne Mannering who was immediately taken with the work and our photographer Graham Beckley took photographs of the exhibits. Churnett Valley Press stepped in to produce the book described on page 78.

Another offer is Rob Birkbeck's *A Picture of a Moment in Time* in which several Society members have an input. It is described on page 9 and there is an order form in the pull-out.

I hope that there will be something of interest to all readers amongst the articles from our regular contributors and five newcomers.

# EDITORIAL   Summer 2000

IT is a great pleasure to present in this issue a profile of Johann Van Leerzem whose name will already be known to readers for his articles about the supply of that basic, taken-for-granted, essential item in our lives, clean water. His late entry into the realms of University guided research and years of study are to be rewarded by the University of Wolverhampton with a well deserved academic award.

In 1991 I took Noel Brettell (Lye born, distinguished Southern African writer, Black Country Personality No. 13 in Vol. 24 No. 4 of *The Blackcountryman*) to the Black Country Museum and he was thrilled to see recreated there examples of the old Black Country he remembered from his childhood from 1908. He had emigrated to Southern Rhodesia in 1930 to teach and observed there a different sort of hardship from that which he had seen in the Black Country. In later correspondence he reflected upon his Museum visit which had been a high point in his rare holiday in Britain, and though many of the exhibits had excited him, on reflection, he thought that it was all too clean. He remembered a poverty stricken, rough, dirty, semi-rustic environment.

Well, of course the Museum is clean. Who would want to visit a dirty museum? For those who want to know what life was really like for many people vivid accounts in books by Kathleen Dayus (about Birmingham) would be enlightening. In this issue, on this theme is a vivid, cheerful account by Roy Cook of what life was really like in a poor post-war Black Country home. I first met Roy in 1948 and after 50 years found him just as cheerful and happy as I remembered him as a 15 year old, and still with fond memories of his happy childhood, tough though life was.

In the interests of authenticity, the author of "Black Country Pits above and below ground and what they were really like" suggested that two tons of horse manure be deposited in the Black Country Museum mine experience to create the true atmosphere. Thankfully that did not happen. Most people prefer to view the sanitised version of old Black Country life as depicted now at the Black Country Living Museum. Realistic accounts of what life was really like for many: earth kitchen floors, rats in the chimney breast, bugs behind the wallpaper, party lavatories, shoe repairs with cardboard, swimming in the canal, are available for those who, after a Museum visit, need to 'complete' the experience.

I hope that all readers will find items to interest them in the personal reminiscences, accounts about our industrial heritage and general items. In the Reviews section there are details of books which I hope will make some members reach for their cheque books, and there are the regular features.

# EDITORIAL   Autumn 2000

THE Society's fruitful association with Sutton Publishing Limited ("Black Country in Old Photographs" series) continues and several more titles will be published before Christmas. In some cases the Society organises a launch, in others we just have a presence when the new book is launched. Either way the Society benefits. Further details will be found in the Pullout and we offer members a service by post for these books at the cover prices.

I have been fortunate always to be able to assemble for each magazine a collection of Black Country articles on a wide variety of topics. In this issue, one article has "made it" a couple of years after receiving it, another immediately upon receipt. It is a matter of balance. The latter article is on a subject close to my heart. Contributed by John Sanders, Chairman of the Friends of Broadfield House Glass Museum, it chronicles the steps taken quietly over nearly two years, to obtain the necessary Church of England authority to do some some "grave robbing". About a month before the work could be done our cover was nearly blown when a correspondent to *The Stourbridge News* drew attention to the objects of the exercise. See page 49.

The December magazine, Vol. 34 No. 1, will be my 50th since succeeding my distinguished predecessor, the late Harold Parsons, who produced 83 issues over 21 years. The next magazine will be a 'Special' of 100 pages to commemorate this particular minor landmark and will include a profile of a nationally known Black Country personality.

# EDITORIAL    Winter 2001

I AM grateful to the Committee for permitting this issue to have 100 pages as it is my 50th magazine since September 1988 when I took over from Harold Parsons who edited the first 83. This coincides with a cover price increase for casual purchasers, only the second price rise in 12 years! Subscribing Society members will not be affected by this increase and readers who are not members of the Black Country Society are urged to join and then to receive their magazines by post or by hand delivery.

Lisa Potts, G.M. our Black Country Personality - No. 50, was awarded the George Medal in the 1997 Honours List for her courage in saving nursery children during an attack on them outside St. Luke's School, Wolverhampton, by a crazed machette wielding man. It is a privilege to carry this brave Black Country girl's story in *The Blackcountryman*. She was scarred for life and recently, four years on, underwent yet another operation on her left hand which was nearly severed in the attack. The respect and affection amongst the general public was demonstrated for me when my wife and I had lunch with her at a country pub during the Summer. Two elderly ladies who were just leaving stopped by our table and stared for a few seconds and one hesitantly asked, "Excuse me . . . but are you . . . . ?" Lisa jumped up and said, "Yes, I'm Lisa Potts", and both of the ladies, totally unknown to her, gave her a hug and a kiss and said, "God Bless You".

For 30 years, since Wordsley Community Association moved to new premises at Wordsley Green I have watched the vacated and thereafter unused former Wordsley Art School and Institute gradually deteriorate. Its demolition which has been going on since September is nearly finished. The provision of this facility in this rural setting as it was then was almost unique. The thinking behind such establishments which developed in Victorian times is covered briefly in Bill Pace's most interesting article, "Technical Education for Craftsmen". His experience was in the metal trades, but from the beginning of the voluntary further education movement, non-metal trades such as glassmaking and pottery in this area were included in the programme. It was the need of the latter to improve in the face of growing foreign competition which led to the founding of Wordsley School of Art, a brief history of which starts on page 73.

An extended book section is included which together with the Pull-out should tempt readers to reach for their cheque books before Christmas. "Book Reviews" includes two substantial accounts, on the Society's new *The Black Country as seen through Antique Maps* – a Survey from 1579 by Eric Richardson, and Tim Cockin's amazing *Staffordshire Encyclopaedia*, now nearly sold out. Every effort will be made to send out orders received, by return of post.

I hope that all readers will find something of interest in my "landmark for me" 50th magazine. I am grateful to the many people who have helped over the years, writers, packers, distributors, publicists, programme organisers, advertisers and others whose collective efforts have consolidated the term **THE BLACK COUNTRY** which was a primary objective of the Society's founders 34 years ago when bureaucrats would have abandoned it.

It is now 13 years since I was invited to become Editor on my retirement from Dudley's Education Service in August 1988. I have asked the Committee to find a successor in 2001 whom I can ease into the position, hence the notice on page 4. I hope to continue to be of some service to the Society for some time, but because of my age, to use a current popular expression, it would be prudent for the Society to look to the future.

Finally, Seasons Greetings to all readers.

25

# EDITORIAL   Spring 2001

FOUR and a half years after the horrific machette attack at St. Luke's Nursery, Wolverhampton in which small children and their nursery nurse, Lisa Potts, G.M. (Black Country Personality No. 50 in Vol. 34 No. 1 of *The Blackcountryman*) were badly injured, Lisa's compensation has been announced. The total figure includes amounts for loss of earnings (nursery nurses are poorly paid), psychological damage (Lisa still suffers), and physical injuries (her most recent operation was only a few weeks ago).

In my profile of Lisa in the Winter magazine I listed some of the immediate hospital repair work thus: 45 stitches in her left hand which was nearly severed, 15 stitches in her right hand, 25 stitches on her back and her skull was chipped by another blow. The injuries element in the compensation package was just £1,000. She described this and the children's compensation as unfair and this sparked off some unjustified criticism in a national tabloid and from a surgeon who attended some of the victims. The latter in a letter to *The Times* stated, "For her injuries she received a sum of money that many would consider substantial. It is sad that she expects more." £1,000 for those injuries – Ridiculous! He also stated that she had written three books, as if that had any bearing on the assessment for injuries. (The profits from the first book were donated to The Acorn Children's Hospice).

Lisa's complaint that the injuries element of the award is not commensurate with their severity has been justified by the news that the Home Secretary has announced that there is to be a shake-up of the compensation scheme for the victims of crime in view of the awards given in this case.

Our Black Country heroine does not deserve the nasty comments, and one hopes that, helped by the tremendous volume of support that she has received, she will treat them with the contempt they deserve.

From its founding in 1966 the Black Country Society has been at the forefront of the campaign to ensure the survival of the term **The Black Country** when some would have preferred to discard it. From time to time *The Blackcountryman* has taken these people to task. Gradually the nickname coined in the mid-19th century has become more generally accepted with the term being used as a prefix for important bodies such as The Black Country Living Museum, The Black Country Metropolitan Boroughs and the Black Country Development Corporation. The number of local businesses using the term in their title runs into three figures. The most recent move to consolidate the name further is by *The Express & Star* which in response to a suggestion by a Society member has adopted as its masthead for the Dudley edition, "Dudley – The Capital of the Black Country."

In this issue Black Country Personality No. 51 is a former colleague in Education, Angus Dunphy who was awarded the O.B.E. in the New Year's Honours List. Honours awarded to two other members are also recorded.

Five new contributors have their articles included in this issue, which together with items from our old established writers and the regular features, will provide something of interest to all readers.

The name of my successor should be announced at the A.G.M. and I shall 'soldier on' until he is ready to assume responsibility.

# EDITORIAL     Autumn 2001

FIVE new contributors' articles are, included in this issue which together with items from our regular writers covers a wide range of topics including a ground breaking one, the first of a series.

Black Country Personality No. 53, Charles Leonard York, a Smethwich born man who became a mountaineer, fell off the Matterhorn and lived, has told me his story of Black Country spirit and the will to live and have a useful life despite being paralysed from the neck down. I hope that sometime during the coming season one branch of the Society at least will have the opportunity of hearing his slide illustrated lecture.

The Society's advantageous association with Sutton Publishing Limited continues in several ways. There is a continuing programme of books about the Black Country to be published, see page 77, and we are again receiving help from that Publisher in the preparation of the Society's 2002 Calendar. The first of the programme's new books is Dr. Paul Collins's superb *Black Country Canals*. The Society provides a postal service for members who may order Sutton Black Country books from the Society at cover price with the Society meeting the postage and packing charge. A reprint of our *Black Country Nurse at Large* by the late Edith Cotterill is imminent and we have two more books in an advanced stage of preparation.

The Black Country Society Living Museum - "Living Museum of the Year - 2001" in *The Good Britain Guide Awards*, continues to develop with exciting additions. There are new schemes afoot, brief details of which are given on pages 68-9, together with a programme of special events in the remainder of 2001. The Society's representative of the Museum Board, Ron Julian, has negotiated with the Museum Administration a "*Two for the Price of One*" offer. Look for the voucher enclosed with this magazine.

This is the 53rd issue of *The Blackcountryman* which I have edited since I succeeded my distinguished predecessor and founder of the magazine, Harold Parsons (he edited 83 issues), on my retirement from Dudley's Education Service exactly 13 years ago. Thus two people have taken "The Premier Magazine of the Black Country" (A Black Country mon doe cry stinkin' fish!) from 1968 into the new millennium.

I notified the Committee that I would like to retire as soon as possible after my 50th magazine and a search was begun to find a successor. Eventually David Cox who joined the Committee a couple of years ago emerged and he will take responsibility for the magazine from the December 2001, issue (Vol. 35 No. 1). Aged 38, David is a graduate of Birmingham University (Ancient History and Archaeology), has obtained an M.A. (O.U.) in History, and is now well into Ph.D. research. He has contributed several fine articles to the magazine on locations and events near his birthplace: Wordsley Brewery, Wordsley Hospital, Amblecote Hall, The Murder at Dunsley Hall and the Roman Camp at Greensforge.

I would like to place on record my sincere thanks to all who have contributed to my retirement hobby being such a satisfying and happy time. So many people have come forward to help in some way or other that pages would be needed to record them all, but they include Officers and members of the Society's Committee, past Presidents and members of the Society, already established and well over 200 new contributors, advertisers and members of the branches, staff at Sutton Publishing and staff of local newspapers.

I must however, mention two people. Jean my wife who has been a constant support and Martyn Round our printer. Like the Church of England with the appointment of a married priest, who gets "two for the 'price' of one" so has the Society with me. Over 13 years, Jean has absorbed the Society's ethos by a process similar to passive smoking. Martyn Round, after more than 50 years at Reliance Printing Works recently retired from business. He was involved with the production of every one of the 136 issues of *The Blackcountryman*, and most of the other Society's publications since the founding, and during my tenure has become a good friend and unofficial assistant editor. His quiet contribution to the Society's progress is inestimable. This was recognised at the 1999 AGM when he was made an Honorary Life Member.

Some of the other work which I have been covering including canvassing for advertisements, delivery to sales outlets recruitment and publicity I shall be continuing and hope to generate additional income so that we may take the magazine further forward.

(Signing off) Stan Hill.
Editor 1988 - 2001.

27

# 2.

# Flying the Flag

The job of an Editor of a society magazine is to keep members abreast of activities they've missed, fundraise, inform members what fellow members are getting up to, and publise the Society. Here is a small selection of these types of articles.

## THE BLACK COUNTRY SOCIETY'S 30th ANNIVERSARY DINNER

A CELEBRATORY dinner to mark the 30th Anniversary of the founding of the Black Country Society was attended by 80 members and guests on 30th April 1997 at the Ward Arms Dudley where the first Annual Dinner was held. Guests included the Mayors and Mayoresses of Dudley, Sandwell and Wolverhampton and the Deputy Mayor and Deputy Mayoress of Walsall, Mr. and Mrs. J. Brimble, Mr. and Mrs. I. Walden, Mrs. Pauline Fletcher and Mr. Cedric Fletcher, Mrs. Maureen Wilkes and Mr. B. Wilkes (Friends of the Museum) and Mrs. Harold Parsons.

Moving the toast, "The Black Country Society" Mr. Ian Walden, O.B.E., Director of the Black Country Living Museum referred to the founders of the Black Country Society who were amongst the earliest campaigners for an industrial museum and to the co-operation between the Museum and the Society which he looked forward to seeing develop. Replying, Mr. John Brimble, J.P. co-founder with Dr. John Fletcher of the Black Country Society, paid tribute to the Society's early pioneers and the present office holders who, building on firm foundations, had brought the Society to its present best ever position. Proposing the toast "Our

Guests" Stan Hill, Chairman, thanked each for honouring the Society with their presence and referred to the late Harold Parsons, founder – Editor of The Blackcountryman who produced 83 magazines in 21 years and whose record of service to the Society is unlikely to be beaten. Gwen Kingsley (Genealogist and twice finalist in the BBC's TV Mastermind) responded on the theme "That was the news that was."

The Society's new President, Mr. Malcolm Lacey, presided and the event was organised by Mr. Ron Julian (Membership Secretary). Music throughout the evening was by Richard Northwood (organ).

# THE FAMILY AND LOCAL HISTORY FAIR

THE third Family and Local History Fair organised by the Black Country Society and Dudley Libraries was held at Dudley Town Hall on Saturday and Sunday, 25th and 26th September 1998. There were 35 exhibitors including local history societies, civic and amenity groups, local authority archives stands, local authors and antiquarian booksellers.

Several special events were staged during the two day event, the first on the Saturday when a new book on Dudley in the Sutton Publishing Ltd. series *Britain in Old Photographs* was launched by Ross Cranston, M.P. for Dudley North and Solicitor General. The authors are Hilary Atkins (Dudley Borough Archivist) and two of her staff, Diane Matthews and Samantha Robins. Ross Cranston spoke of the value of this series of books in local studies and drew attention to some of the photographs in the new book which particularly attracted him. Mrs. Atkins gave the background and David Radmore (Borough Librarian) announced that the authors had decided to devote all royalties to the work of the Dudley Archive Service.

On Sunday Mrs. Sylvia Everitt exhibited her 10 tapestry panels depicting 1,000 years of Staffordshire life and gave talks on how she had set about the work which had taken her five years. The Black Country is well represented in the panels – see front cover and article on pages 17 to 22.

On Sunday afternoon four experts attended for an 'Antiques Identified' event. Charles Hanmer compered the event and introduced Henry Sandon, a BBC 'Antiques Roadshow' star, Charles Hajdamach, Dudley's Principal Museums Officer and glass expert, Simon Davies and Stuart Whittaker of Fellows & Sons, Auctioneers, Hockley. During the afternoon over 100 items were identified and valued and £163 raised for the Black Country Living Museum's fund for equipping the proposed new interpretation centre (Rolfe Street Baths Project).

On both days there were video presentations of old films of Black Country life compiled by Dr. Paul Collins and Mrs. Gwen Kingsley, genealogist, gave consultations. The Black Country Town Crier, Percy Simmonds, advertised the event around the town and made proclamations as necessary.

It is proposed to stage a similar event in the year 2000.

# Black Country Society AGM March 2002

THE 35th Annual General Meeting of the Black Country Society was held at the Black Country Living Museum on 27th March 2002. Stan Hill was appointed President for the ensuing year, succeeding his old school friend, Ray Weston of the Wyre Forest Branch of the Black Country Society.

The two men became friends in 1940 when they first attended King Edward's School, Stourbridge, after winning scholarships. They followed similar careers: Teacher Training College, 1946-8, instructors in the Royal Army Education Corps, 1948-50, advanced education courses at Birmingham University in the 1950s and teaching until retirement, Ray 16 years ago from the Headmastership of Cradley High School and Stan from being Warden of Dudley Teachers' Centre at Himley Hall and Portway. Both have devoted much of their retirement to the Black Country Society. Ray started the Wyre Forest Branch at Kidderminster with Joyce his wife, and Stan as Editor of *The Blackcountryman* from 1988 until September 2001, having edited 53 quarterly issues with a 5-year stint as Chairman in addition.

From the Wyre Forest Branch, Ray formed the Black Country Concert Party, *'Cum Sing Wi' We'*, which in the past 13 years has raised over £60,000 for charity.

Stan continues to serve the Society with support work for *The Blackcountryman:* advertising, distribution, writing, publicity, recruitment and editing other Society publications.

The old school pals have the satisfaction of seeing the Black Country Society in its strongest ever position, with over 2,600 members.

## The Black Country Society
## Queen's Golden Jubilee Commemoration Fund

TO mark the Queen's Golden Jubilee the Black Country Society has set aside the sum of £6,000, from which 8 worthy causes will be given cheques. Stan Hill announced details at the A.G.M. which was attended by representatives of the first two beneficiaries. He presented a cheque for £1,000 to Mr Ian Walden OBE, Director of the Black Country Living Museum towards the maintenance of the recently acquired IMI Marston Historic Vehicle Collection (see article on pages 67-9). Mr Walden thanked the Society for its continuing support. Stan also presented a cheque to an archivist from Wolverhampton City Archives towards the cost of the purchase of a 1713 Newcomen diary in connection with a Bilston installation of that date. Again thanks were expressed.

# BLACK COUNTRY SOCIETY 36th A.G.M.

SEVENTY members attended the 36th Annual General Meeting held on 26th March at the Black Country Living Museum when Stan Hill, retiring President, referred to the Society's continued progress over the past year and to the success of the four new books published since last September. The Society's Queen's Golden Jubilee Commemoration Fund has made donations to several causes and there are more in the pipeline. Attendances at the six branches have increased and in an average Autumn month there is an aggregate attendance of about 10% of the membership. Last year's excursions programme was oversubscribed. Reference was made to the world-wide interest in the Society generated by the new website and to the *The Blackcountryman* editor's work to improve the magazine further.

Ron Julian, who was Membership Secretary for 12 years and has acted as Treasurer for the past eight months and is the Society's representative on the board of the Black Country Living Museum, was appointed President for the ensuing year. Ron, a retired civil servant, is a founder member and Treasurer of Kingswinford History Society and co-author of two old photograph books of Kingswinford and Wall Heath. He is also a volunteer at Mary Stevens Hospice, as is his wife, Barbara, retired Head of Brockmoor Primary School. He enjoys travelling and supports Aston Villa. In his acceptance address the new President paid tribute to the work over the past fifteen years of the retiring President, ably supported by his wife. He expressed the hope that members would continue to support the Museum in every way possible.

Charles Hanmer (Chairman) presented a Life Membership scroll to long-serving Committee member and Past-President, Mrs Vi Whetton, on her retirement. After the interval, Society member the Reverend Carol Hathorne gave a lively, entertaining address based on her book *Slurry & Strawberries – A Tipton Childhood* published by the Society in October 2002.

*Vi Whetton receiving her Life Membership scroll from l. to r., Ron Julian (President), Stan Hill (retiring President), and Charles Hanmer (Chairman).*

# THE BLACK COUNTRY SOCIETY'S QUEEN'S GOLDEN JUBILEE COMMEMORATION FUND

IN early 2002 the Black Country Society responded to a call made to local societies to do something to commemorate the Queen's Golden Jubilee by setting aside some £7,000 from which to assist projects across the Black Country to mark the special occasion. Financial assistance was given to Wolverhampton Archive Centre, The Friends of Dudley Archive Service, The Dudley Geological Collection, The Black Country Living Museum and West Bromwich Civic Society. In addition up to 100 copies of three of the Society's recently published reference books, each with a commemorative book plate, were donated to schools, libraries, colleges, archive centres etc.

At the November 2003 monthly meeting of the Society at the Black Country Living Museum the final major contribution from the fund was made, £2,000 to the University of Wolverhampton to assist a Doctoral degree student studying a Black Country subject. All the arrangements for this student are in the hands of the University and the Society hopes that this will be the beginning of a useful association between one of the oldest voluntary local history societies and the newest university covering the area.

Furthermore, to help students with their Black Country studies the Society is donating to the University a complete set of the 144 published issues of their quarterly magazine *The Blackcountryman,* which contain a unique collection of some 2,000 substantial articles on all aspects of the Black Country, and associated material.

*Left to right:*
Stan Hill (Editor of The Blackcountryman *1988-2001)Mr Ron Julian (Society President 2003-4), Mr Charles Hanmer (Chairman), Dr Sarah Capitanio, (Co-ordinator of the Postgraduate Research Programmes), Brian Dakin (PhD student involved), Tony Copson (Society Vice-Chairman).
*Photograph by Graham Beckley.*

SEATTLE DOWNTOWN NEWS

Seattle Woman

Vol. 6 No.36  Established 1988  FREE

September 6, 1993

## INSIDE Black Country Artist in Seattle

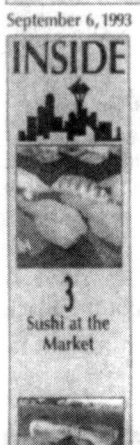

Paul Bloomer, a young artist from England will open as guest artist at The Weathered Wall on Tuesday, September 7th.

Bloomer, born and raised in England's "Black Country", an industrial area in the West Midlands, depicts the frustration of economic decline through his paintings.

The "Black Country" earned its nickname in the 19th century due to the enormous amount of coal mines and iron blast furnaces in operation there.

In the early 1980s the major industrial areas faced economic collapse. The industrial heritage of the "Black Country" was demolished overnight and unemployment was at its highest since the 1930s.

*See Artist on page 5*

Paul Bloomer will open as guest artist at The Weathered Wall (1923 5th Ave) on Tuesday, September 7th.

3

Sushi at the Market

SSF Underway

# FLYING THE FLAG IN THE U.S.A.

AT the invitation of a friend, Paul Bloomer, who featured in the last issue of 'The Blackcountryman', spent his Summer 1993 vacation in Seattle, California. He spent a few weeks there working in a restaurant and when he had saved sufficient money rented a small studio for a month. Paul was invited to be guest artist for a month at Seattle's Weathered Wall Gallery on 5th Avenue. There he exhibited his Summer production of drawings and prints supplemented by work which he had sent over from his home in Pensnett.

The 'Seattle Downtown News' partly reproduced above, carried the following:

Paul Bloomer, a young artist from England will open as guest artist at the Weathered Wall on Tuesday 7th September. Born and raised in England's "Black Country", an industrial area in the West Midlands, Bloomer depicts the frustration of economic decline through his paintings.

The Black Country earned its nickname in the 19th century due to the enormous amount of coal mines and iron blast furnaces in operation there. In the 1980s the major industrial areas faced economic collapse. The industrial heritage of the Black Country was demolished overnight and unemployment was at its highest since the 1930s.

Paul left school in the early 1980s and began drawing when he was 20 years old. The exhibition will feature drawings and prints from the Black Country as well as work inspired by his stay in Seattle.

33

# 3.

# A selection of stories and reports

Stan's contributions to *The Blackcountryman* feature pages go back to 1981, with 'Working on the Railway – Aged 12!' (in fact his earliest contribution to *The Blackcountryman*). They continued into, and beyond, his Editorship. The following is a broad selection, including an article Stan wrote for *The Lady* magazine, which did not appear in *The Blackcountryman*, and few will have seen it.

The poem 'The Foolish People' was contributed by The Revd. K. Tibbetts of Prestatyn. It appeared anonymously in *The Dudleian* in the 1950s, but was in fact by a walking companion of Revd. K. Tibbetts in the 1930s and 1940s.

Stan's pseudonym, Bert Barr, was used when contributions were a bit thin on the ground, and it was considered unseemly for the Editor's name to keep appearing as a byline (there! – the secret's out). Bert is short for Albert, Stan's first name, and Barr is the Old Celtic for a hill!

# From Brierley Hill to British Columbia

## by

### STAN HILL

Warden, Dudley Teachers' Centre

THIS year, the City of Nanaimo, Vancouver Island, British Columbia, celebrates its centenary. Twenty years before its being granted city status in 1874, 24 miners and their families had left the Black Country to start a new life and had founded a settlement there.

A few years earlier, coal had been discovered on Vancouver Island, and in 1852, the Nanaimo area, where more seams were discovered, was taken over by the Hudson's Bay Company.

The company decided to bring out skilled miners and on 20 March, 1854, appointed George Robinson of Eardington Colliery, Bridgnorth, ' Manager of the Company's Coal Works on Vancouver Island.' Robinson was asked to engage 20 colliers from his area and his letter of 3 May, 1854 to the company notes:

> " On Monday, I met the colliers at Mr. William Baker's Swan Inn, Buckpool, Nr. Brierley Hill, and found that only some four or five of the original list were then willing to go. I, however, had used precaution to prevent disappointment and sent the cryer from Dudley through one or two villages in the district informing the miners of my wanting a few miners to go to America, the result was I succeeded in obtaining the number required, objecting to many who were not eligible—or who could not produce me satisfactory testimonials." (H.B.S. Arch. A10/35 Fo 305d.)

The contract for the miners to sign stipulated that a man was bound for five years as a working collier in the mines on Vancouver Island. A loan of £15 was to be made, to be repaid after one year. His own and his family's expenses to the point of embarkation were to be paid, and their passage and food during the voyage. On board ship, he was to be paid 2/6d. a day provided he made himself useful as a labourer, but he was not required to go aloft.

Upon arrival at Nanaimo, he was to build himself wooden accommodation. The wages were to be £78 a year, payable in monthly instalments, for which he was required to work 10 hours a day, on the surface or underground, wages to be forfeited if he absented himself. If, after five years he did not wish to remain in Nanaimo, or if he died in the meantime, then he, his wife and family, or his widow and family, would be provided by the Hudson's Bay Company with free passage and rations back to England.

There was nothing unusual about emigrating in 1854, for in the ten previous years, nearly 2½ million people had done so from the British

35

The Princess Royal. An impression by Miss M. P. Smith, Dudley Teachers' Centre

Isles, and in that year a further third of a million emigrated. With such numbers departing the total population in 1851 was approximately 21 million—most adults would have heard about the opportunities overseas. In fact, the 1851 census returns for Dudley record several wives whose husbands had ' gone to America.' Of those who had emigrated from 1844-1853, approximately 90% had gone to North America, the journey taking 12½ days by steam packet, or more likely 4-7 weeks by sailing vessel at a cost of £3-£4 a head.

What was unusual about the Nanaimo emigrants was the fact that their journey took nearly six months as they had to sail round Cape Horn.

The grim conditions of the mid-19th century led to the mass exodus. Most emigrated for regular food and in hope. The little group of Black Country miners must have pondered deeply over whether or not to ' sign up.' Would they ever reach their destination? Would they ever return to Brierley Hill? Were the risks worth taking for the prospect of a better life?

Eventually 23 miners signed up, and, together with wives and children, making up a party of 83, left the district to arrive in London on 2 June, 1854.

36

According to the records, the following were those from Brierley Hill who embarked:

BAKER, George, wife, son Daniel and daughter Hester.
BAKER, John and wife.
BEVILOCKWAY, Joseph L., wife, sons Moses and George, daughter Catherine.
BIGGS, John and wife.
BULL, George, wife and daughter.
DUNN, Daniel and wife.
GANNER, Elijah, wife, sons Joseph and Elijah and daughters Sarah and Eliza.
GOUGH, Edwin, wife, sons Samuel and Reuben and daughter Jane Ellen.
HARRISON, William and wife.
HAWKES, Thomas, wife, son James and daughter Jane Ellen.
INCHER, William and wife.
JONES, Thomas and wife.
LOWNDES, Thomas and wife.
MALPASS, John, wife, son James and daughter Eliza.
MAKIN, John, wife, sons John and Frederick.
MILLER, Matthew, wife, daughters Maria and Polly.
RICHARDSON, Richard and wife.
RICHARDSON, John, wife, sons Peter and Andrew and daughter Esther.
ROBINSON, George, wife, son Victor, daughter Amanda and maid.
SAGE, Jesse, wife, sons William and George and daughter Selena.
THOMPSON, John and wife.
TURNER, Richard and daughter Christiana.
WEBB, Joseph and wife.
YORK, Thomas, wife and daughter Phoebe.

Origins of the emigrants included: Wordsley, Brierley Hill, Pensnett, Bromley, Commonside, Brockmoor, Kingswinford, Dudley.

The pioneers embarked on the new Hudson Bay Company barque, the Princess Royal, 700 tons, on 2 June. They had no berths or cabins, since they were steerage passengers and had to make themselves comfortable as best they could in the main hold at the bottom of the ship. At 4 a.m. on 3 June, the ship left East India dock.

It was an eventful voyage as the following extracts from the ship's log, kept by Charles Gale, First Mate, show:

July   1   8 a.m. Mrs. Clarke's baby died. It has been ill ever since it has been on board. 5.30 p.m. Buried Mrs. Clarke's baby.

July 16   10.30 a.m. Divine Service was performed with all hands in attendance except the sick. John Baker's wife was taken with a fit while in church, taken out.

**STRIKE BY MINERS**

July 29   (Landsmen complained of rice and some refused to work pending the inquiry into the matter). The 10 Norwegians proceeded to their work as usual, and also the landsmen that had been picked out as idlers, viz: Thomas York and Jno. Malpass. Serving out stores with the 3rd officer, Wm. Harrison and Daniel Dunn assist to Cook, Geo. Bull assisting the Steward and Jesse Sage attending on the stock.

July 30   Landsmen returned to work. Names of those that refused as under:— George Baker, John Baker, Matthew Miller, John Meaking, William Incher, Joseph Webb, Richard Turner, Richard Richardson, John Richardson, Thomas Jones, Elijah Ganner, John Thompson, Thomas Lownds, Thomas Hawkes, Joseph Beckilockway, John Biggs and Edwin Gough.

37

## ROUNDING THE HORN

The rounding of the Horn was accomplished in mid-winter after a severe buffeting and as the ship nosed north, the weather improved as they approached Hawaii.

Sept. 21   Buried Malpass child with usual ceremony.

Sept. 24   We had a birth this afternoon in a very great haste; at 10.00 a.m. woman was on deck washing; at 3.30 p.m. she was confined. Mrs. J. Baker.

Sept. 30   Mrs. Sage one emigrant confined this being the 2nd birth.

Oct. 20   Arrived Honolulu.

Oct. 28   Mrs. Incher has been confined this morning and is dangerous ill. At 5 p.m. Mrs. Incher died but the baby still lives, also a child belonging to Elijah Ganner died about the same time; the undertaker was immediately sent for to measure and make coffins for them both. At 10.30 p.m. the coffins was brought on board and the two dead bodies taken on shore.

Oct. 29   At 8.30, Mr. Robinson with five more of the people went on shore to burie the two corps.

Oct. 31   Left Honolulu.

Nov. 8   At 3h p.m. William Incher's Infant died, the Mother of which was buried at Honolulu. At 8h 30m p.m. the Infant was throwen over board and no more notice taken of it than if it had been a ded cat.

Nov. 13   5h 30m Buried the child belonging to Richard Richardson. It was found at 3h 30m this morning by the side of its Mother, the usual Cerimoney was performed by the Capt.

Nov. 23   Anchored in the harbor of Esquimalt.

Nov. 24   The Robinsons and party has been busey packing all the day, and getting all ready to leave To Morrow by the Steamer.

Nov. 25   Landed Mr. Clarke and Mr. Robinson's servant. At 4.30 p.m. the schooner Recovery was brought alongside for the passengers put every Thing into her. At 7 p.m. She halld off and came to Anchor with the passengers for the cole mines on board. The Norwegians still Remain on board.

Nov. 28   (An extract from a letter sent by Chief Factor Douglas to H. B. Co. London.) The passengers per the Princess Royal have all been landed and Mr. Robinson with the Miners and their families were sent by the Beaver and Recovery to Colvilletown on the 26th inst. with a good supply of potatoes and fresh meat.

On embarkation there were 83 in the Brierley Hill party of whom 77 landed. (The following died en route: Thomas Lowndes, Mrs. Wm. Incher, infants of Mrs. Bull, Mrs. Malpass, Mrs. Ganner and Mrs. Richardson).

Two days after the arrival, Mrs. James Bevilockway gave birth to a daughter, Julia.

The newcomers soon settled in and there is no record of any of them returning to Britain, although Thomas York left to open a mine for an American company, leaving there for the Fraser river gold rush.

### Recent contacts with Nanaimo

Details of this emigration started coming to light in November, 1954 when the Nanaimo section of the British Columbia Historical Society wrote to Brierley Hill's ' Mayor or Municipal Authority ' saying that it was intended to mark the centenary by a re-enacting of the landing in the costume of the period. The Chairman of the Council (Councillor Eric

38

Gibbons) responded with a cable.

Some months later, the vice-president of the British Columbia Historical Society, Mr. J. Walley, visited Brierley Hill and was taken on a conducted tour of the district by the writer, then Chairman of the Council. Mr .Walley expressed disappointment that no descendants or relatives of the pioneers had been traced.

There was a further link in 1965 when Mr. and Mrs. Frank Martin visited Nanaimo and carried a good will message from the local Council. They were the first recorded visitors from the place of origin of the pioneers, and received V.I.P. treatment whilst there.

**Local Schools Projects**

The local collection at Brierley Hill Library contains a record of the links between the town and Nanaimo. Much of this has been photocopied, stencilled and entered in the Resources Bank at Dudley Teachers' Centre, so being easily accessible to teachers wishing to use it.

Three teachers at The Brook Primary School, Wordsley, Mrs. B. Hill, Mrs. M. Nash and Mr. G. Nunn, using multiple copies of the Nanaimo material supplied by the Teachers' Centre, developed a team-teaching project with two top classes. Their researches enabled them to write booklets so that the children could study interesting lines arising from the emigration, such as: 19th century Brierley Hill, Social and Working Conditions; The Journey; Discovery; Exploration and Settlement of N. America; North American Indian; The development of Nanaimo; Emigration.

The Teachers' Centre produced the booklets for the project and these are now available for other schools in the Borough wishing to use them.

Since the Teachers' Centre interest in Nanaimo has become known, several teachers and visitors have disclosed that they have been there, some on war service, but were unaware of the local connection.

Recently, Mrs. A. J. Preece, widow of a former well known Brierley Hill business man, visited her son in Vancouver and paid a visit to Vancouver Island. She spent an afternoon at the Brook Primary School recently and gave the children an interesting eye witness account of Nanaimo. Amongst the photographs she showed was one taken in that city near a ' Brierley Hill ' road sign.

This interesting episode in our local history is commemorated by a road off Bromley Lane being named Nanaimo Way, the residents of which will soon be invited by The Brook Primary School, Headmaster, Mr. G. Hodgson, to visit the school to see the exhibition based on the project.

From researches now proceeding, it is hoped that new information will come to light about the event.

(*Sources: Material in the Brierley Hill Library Collection, ' Passage to America' by Terry Coleman, The Hudson's Bay Company who gave permission for the inclusion of the extract from George Robinson's letter in this article.*)

# WORDSLEY SCHOOL OF ART

by

Stan Hill

MR. Benjamin F. Mason who qualified as a schoolmaster at the Worcester Diocesan Training College at Saltley, Birmingham, in 1878, opened the Brettell Lane School under Kingswinford School Board in a Wesleyan Methodist Chapel there on 21st August 1882. Within a year, a committee of the school met (on 21st June 1883) to select a site at Audnam for a new school. November 7th 1884 was the last day at the temporary premises which were superseded by Wordsley Board Schools in Brook Street he opening ceremony for which was held on 10th November 1884.

A Wordsley Night Art Class had been established in Wordsley in the 1860s, possibly held at Wordsley Institute which had been established in a former Congregational Church situated near the bottom of Wordsley High Street at its junction with Brewery Street (now Brierley Hill Road). On 1st September 1885 Kingswinford School Board gave permissiion for a night school to be held at the Brook Street Schools and the first night school Art class was held on 28th September 1885. A week later a class in Science was established.

Mr. Owen Gibbons who had been Head of a school of art at Coalbrookdale came to live in Wordsley and he took the night school Art class and Mr. B. F. Mason took the Science class. There was soon a large attendance at the classes and this was maintained. From the beginning the studies in both Art and Science classes, which were held under the auspices of the City and Guilds of London Institute, were related to the local glass and pottery industries. Successes in the national examinations soon came with their first Silver Medal in 1898, a Gold Medal and a Bronze Medal in 1899 and another Silver Medal in 1900.

About this time Mr. Gibbons was informed that the night classes could no longer be held in the Board Schools and it was feared that this progessive long establish facility would be lost to Wordsley. However, Mr. Gibbons was able to obtain the use of the Wordsley Institute building and this arrangement was approved by a committee which included Messrs. W. O. Bowen, Frederick Carder and William Northwood. The 'advanced' students also approved although it seems that they were invited to receive their instruction at Mr. Gibbons's private residence 'The White House'.

The Wordsley Mechanics Institute was established in a typical small early 19th century disused chapel which by this time also housed a private school run by a Mr. B. Johnson. The Wordsley Conservative Club also used the building.

The School Board's decision not to continue housing the night classes seems strange for on 2nd October 1893 permission for night classes in Cookery, Gardening and Wood Turning was given.

Staffordshire County Council, created by the Local Government Act of 1888, had funds available ("whiskey money") which were available for the development of technical education. A Mr. Jones, the Director of the County Councul department involved, visited Wordsley in 1891 and recommended the building of a new School of Art and Institute as the only way forward to meet adequately the needs

*The former Congregational chapel, c1830, which became Wordsley Institute.*
*The inscription over the doorway read 'Wordsley Art Class'.*

of the district. A Building Committee was formed with Messrs. B. F. Mason and W. O. Bowen as hon. secretaries. Mr. Thomas Robinson was appointed Architect to the project.

From the Architect's plans Mr. Owen Gibbons produced a perspective drawing which headed the subscription appeal which was distributed in 1892

The following subscription list was published in 1897:

| | £ | s. | d. | | £ | s. | d. |
|---|---|---|---|---|---|---|---|
| | | | | Brought forward | 519 | 7 | 1 |
| Messrs. Stuart & Sons | 110 | 0 | 0 | W. Davidson | 1 | 1 | 0 |
| W.H. Richardson, | 105 | 0 | 0 | T.W. Robinson, The Cedars | 1 | 1 | 0 |
| Further | 25 | 0 | 0 | W. Northwood, Glass Designer | 1 | 1 | 0 |
| Messrs. W. & E. Webb | 100 | 0 | 0 | S. Hill, Cabinet Maker | 1 | 1 | 0 |
| H.G. Richardson & Sons | 10 | 10 | 0 | E.C. Whitney, Draper, High St. | 1 | 1 | 0 |
| J. Northwood, Art Director, S & W | 10 | 10 | 0 | J.T.Hambury, Cutter, George St. | 1 | 1 | 0 |
| Rev.J.J.Slade, Rector of Wordsley | 10 | 0 | 0 | C.H.Parsons, New St. | 1 | 1 | 0 |
| H. Smith | 10 | 0 | 0 | S. Smith | 1 | 0 | 0 |
| Gibbons, Hinton & Co. (Tiles) | 10 | 0 | 0 | J.R. Taylor | | 10 | 6 |
| Miss Richardson | 5 | 0 | 0 | Mrs.Whitehouse, Butcher, | | 10 | 6 |
| Further | 1 | 0 | 0 | C. Collins, | | 10 | 6 |
| J.S.Williams, | 5 | 5 | 0 | C. Davies, | | 10 | 6 |
| Messrs.Webb, Shaw & Co., | 5 | 5 | 0 | S. Elcock, High St. | | 10 | 0 |
| Messrs. Ketley Brick Co., | 5 | 5 | 0 | J.B. Wright, Grocer, | | 10 | 0 |
| O.G.Meatyard, Audnam Cottage | 5 | 5 | 0 | S. Horsfall, Mill Hoiuse | | 10 | 0 |

41

| | | | | | | |
|---|---|---|---|---|---|---|
| Boulton & Mills, Audnam Glasswks | 5 | 0 | 0 | J.Hill, Mill Lane, | 10 | 0 |
| J.Guest & Sons | 5 | 0 | 0 | E. Hand, | 10 | 0 |
| L.S.Hingley & Sons, Albert Glaswks | 5 | 0 | 0 | H. Freer, | 10 | 0 |
| F. Carder, Glass designer, Schl.Head | 5 | 0 | 0 | T. Richardson, | 10 | 0 |
| Thos. Robinson, Stream Rd., K'ford. | 5 | 0 | 0 | A.P. Richardson, | 10 | 0 |
| J. Corbett, | 3 | 3 | 0 | C. Blackshaw, Schl.Attend.Off. | 7 | 6 |
| G.K. Harrison, Firebrick Manfctr. | 3 | 3 | 0 | B.Johnson, Parish Clerk/Confect. | 7 | 6 |
| W,H. Stuart, Bank House, | 3 | 3 | 0 | Miss Phibbs | 7 | 6 |
| D. Grainger, John Street, | 3 | 3 | 0 | W.P. Richardson, | 7 | 6 |
| Mrs. Roose, | 3 | 3 | 0 | J.Sutton & Nephew, Butchers | 5 | 0 |
| Guest Brothers, | 3 | 0 | 0 | E.Gill, Butcher, | 5 | 0 |
| B.F. Mason, Head of Board School, | 2 | 12 | 0 | J.F. McCourt, Grocer, High St. | 5 | 0 |
| Ten Students | 2 | 5 | 0 | H.Swain, Head of The Glynne Sch. | 5 | 0 |
| R.Deakin, Head of KESchl. S'bridge | 2 | 2 | 0 | W. Clark, | 5 | 0 |
| A.J.H. Richardson, Asst. Overseer, | 2 | 2 | 0 | D.W. Hammond, | 5 | 0 |
| J. Lycett, | 2 | 2 | 0 | W. Davies, | 5 | 0 |
| T. &. J. Woodall | 2 | 2 | 0 | Will Meredith, Surveyor, KRDC. | 5 | 0 |
| Further | 10 | 6 | | Jos. Hill, | 5 | 0 |
| F. Stuart Jnr., | 2 | 2 | 0 | Geo. Thompson, Platts Cresc. | 5 | 0 |
| Miss Hodgetts, Wordsley House, | 2 | 2 | 0 | Mrs. Reading, | 5 | 0 |
| O. Gibbons, The White House, | 2 | 2 | 0 | Mr. & Mrs. Worrall, | 5 | 0 |
| Richardson Employees | 2 | 2 | 0 | Amounts under 5s | 3 8 | 6 |
| J. Jordan, | 1 | 1 | 0 | | | |
| W.H.A. Richardson, | 1 | 1 | 0 | | | |
| B. Richardson, | 1 | 1 | 0 | | | |

Total   £543 14 1

Mr. F. Stuart of Stuart and Sons, old established Wordsley glass manufacturers gave £110 and the Science and Art Department (Government) granted £348, £275 came in two payments from Staffordshire County Council. About half of the cost of the first part of the scheme, £1,616 came from local contributions. Of this total £350 was paid for the site to Mr. F. Stuart, owner of the old Institute.

In 1893 Mr. Gibbons resigned as Headmaster of the school and Mr. Frederick Carder who had been a glass designer at Stevens & Williams's since 1882 was promoted from being second master to the vacancy. Brockmoor born Frederick Carder was the second son of Caleb Carder, earthenware manufacturer of the Leys Pottery, Brockmoor. After leaving the family pottery Frederick became a protege of John Northwood I, the famous re-discoverer of the lost Roman art of cameo glass making. Fred. had achieved great success in the national examinations and was awarded a Silver Medal in 1888, a Gold Medal in 1889 and an Art Master's Certificate in 1901 from which time he took Art classes at Wordsley. He was invited to design two frontage embellishments for the new Art School, one of

*Brook Street Board School.*

which, representing Industry, was a female figure holding a replica of the Portland Vase. He also designed the magnificent floral relief on the archway above the entrance to the building. When the extension was built in 1907, Fred, was well established at the Steuben Glassworks, Corning, New York, and his younger brother George added two more matching terra cotta panels with relief figures.

Queen Victoria's Diamond Jubilee year, 1897, gave inspiration to many local committees to consider some form of commemoration of this unique event and in Wordsley, the Rector, the Rev. J. J. Slade, M.A., chaired a meeting in the National (Church) Schools to consider the matter. After lengthy discussion it was unanimously decided to adopt the building of the Art Schcool and Institute as the Diamond Jubilee memorial for Wordsley. This decision was crucial to the Art School project and brought in a further donation of £196 from Mr. W. H. Richardson.

By 1898 matters had progressed to the level at which a stone laying ceremony could be arranged. The Building Committee met under the chairmanship of the Rev. J. J. Slade, M.A. on 24th June 1898 to finalise the details for the event to be held a few days later on Monday 27th June 1898. Also present at this meeting were Messrs. W. H. A. Richardson, Samuel Elcock, W. Husselbee, Thomas Woodall, William Northwood, W. H. P. Richardson, W. H. Stuart, A. Harrison Hill, B. Richardson, A. J. H. Richardson, Samuel Shotton and the Hon. Secretaries B. F. Mason and Fred. Carder.

Lieut-Colonel W. G. Webb, J.P. performed the stone laying ceremony after which the guests adjourned to the Drill Hall (now the Richardson Hall) for a concert. The guests included Mr. Thomas Turner representing Staffordshire County Council.

43

The Official Opening of the 'New Art School' and Art Exhibition was held on 6th February 1899. The Lord Lieutenant of Staffordshire, the Earl of Dartmouth, accompanied by the Himley Troop of the Queen's Own Royal Regiment of Yeomanry officially opened the building and was presented with a silver key by the Architect, on behalf of the Committee. The building was then handed over to the Trustees. The guests who had been requested to wear uniform or official dress where appropriate were then entertained to lunch in the National Schools. At 3 p.m. there was a procession to the Drill Hall in Lawnswood Road for the formal opening of the associated Art Exhibition.

The Committee kept alive the idea of completing the building according to the original plans and received a great boost in 1903 with a bequest of £748 from the estate of Mrs. Phoebe Carter (fomerly Miss Phoebe North of The Cliff, Buckpool). There was a further grant of £554 from Staffordshire County Council and £100 raised locally and on 24th October 1906 Miss Martha Richardson of Wordsley Hall laid the memorial stone set in the wall on the right hand side of the entrance porch, opposite the stone laid by Lt. Col. Webb eight years previously.

The Official Opening of the extension by Alderman J. T. Homer, Chairman of Staffordshire Education Committee was held on Monday evening 16th September 1907. Mr. Owen Gibbons C.C. presided (the enthusiastic previous Chairman, the Rev. J. J. Slade, M.A., Rector of Wordsley had died). He was an appropriate choice to succeed the Rev. Slade for it was he who first conceived the value of such a school to Wordsley. Amongst the distinguished guests were Mr. A. Staveley Hill, M.P. and Mrs. Hill, Professor Turner of Birmingham University who, as a Staffordshire County Council official, had attended the stone laying ceremony for

*The first half of the Art School project was officially opened on 6th February 1899.*

44

*Frederick Carder's two terra-cotta panels which decorated the frontage of the first part of the Art School at first floor level. Left: Art. Right: Industry.*

the first phase of the building, Alderman John Addison, Rev. R. H. Streeton, Vicar of St. Mary's, Kingswinford), Revs. H. A. Hill (Rector of Wordsley), T. Mirams (Wollaston), Messrs. B. Richardson (Vice-chairman of the Committee), W. H. A. Richardson, G. F. James, C. Dudley, (Hon. Sec. to the Committee), Thomas Woodall (Treasurer), B. F. Mason (Secretary to the Building Committee), Daniel Norwood, C. C. (Brockmoor), J. M. Wynne (Secretary to the Dudley Education Committee), Thomas Williams (Chairman of the Brierley Hill Higher Education Committee), F. Webb, C. C. (Chairman of Quarry Bank Urban District Council), J. J. Eccleston (Chairman of Kingswinford Rural District Council), D. Clark, J.P., G. Meanley, George Carder (art master), E. C. Whitney (Wordsley draper and milliner and funeral director), W. H. Stuart, J. H. Smith, J. H. Collett (Headmaster of the National Schools), A. J. H. Richardson, W. Fullwood, F. Fellows, C. C., J. J. Appleby (Secretary to the Glasscutters' Society), H. Whitney, F. Gibbons, G. S. Hingley, B. Williams, John Whitworth, H. Swain (Headmaster of the Glynne School), S. Skelding, S. Hill, Jnr., Mrs. B. Richardson, Misses N. and M. E. Richardson, Miss Oliver (Cookery Mistress), Mr. J. S. Williams-Thomas (Stevens & Williams, Brierley Hill), Mr. G. F. James (Clerk to Kingswinford Rural District Council and representing the late Mrs. Phoebe Carter).

It was announced at the ceremony that Mr. W. H. Richardson of Glasgow, formerly of Wordsley, had made a further donation to ensure that the building was free from debt.

45

# THE BUILDING

A Kingswinford firm with a base in Market Street. Messrs. George Meanley & Son, was the main contractor. Ketley Brick Co. Ltd. (Managing Director: W. T. Skelding) supplied the bricks and Messrs. Hill & Smith Ltd. of Brierley Hill donated the iron gates for the entrance.

On the ground floor of the completed building was a well equipped Handicrafts Room with eight specially constructed double benches each with a set of ordinary tools, and an Elementary Art and Science Room. On the first floor was the Cookery Centre and an Advanced Art Room. On the second floor was a suite of rooms for instruction in glass manufacture, a Chemistry Laboratory, a Lecture Room and a Furnace Room. Previously the tuition had been theoretical only, hereafter the practical side could be demonstrated and experienced.

There was provision for a weekly attendance of 120 Science and Art students, 96 Handicrafts students and 180 Cookery students.

Equipment suppliers included Addison & Co. of Wellington (cupboards and benches), Fisher and Co. of West Bromwich (desks), Gleave & Son of Manchester (benches and tools) and Jabez Attwood (the heating system).

# THE DEMOLITION

As a programme of new schools building in the 1930s, in the wake of the Haddow Report (1926), better facilities became available at the new 'Senior Schools' and gradually, Wordsley Art School, a leader in its day, was no longer required for its original purpose. However, the handsome building was made available as a community centre and as Wordsley Community Centre became the centre of village life accommodating a wide variety of clubs and activities.

*Mr. W. H. Richardson of Glasgow, formerly of Wordsley, from a portrait at Broadfield House Glass Museum.*

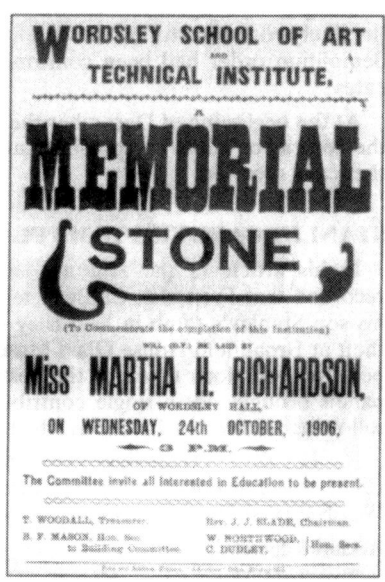

*A poster advertising the stone laying.*

46

*The completed Art School.*

By the late 1950s the Community Association found that the premises were inadequate for its growing programme and pressed for a new building. After the new community centre was opened about 25 years ago the former Art School was closed and not used again. No body, public or private, could find a use for the building in its dangerous location. In 2000 a figure of £1 million was suggested as the likely cost of restoring the derelict edifice. As soon as it was announced that a demolition order had been confirmed thieves came overnight and stole the iron gates.

At the beginning of December the demolition was nearly finished. An appeal to the contractor about the possible saving of the two foundation stones was sympathetically received.

## STANLEY CARDER'S TOMB PLAQUES

In his article in the Autumn issue of The Blackcountryman, John Sanders recorded that Frederick Carder's terra-cotts 'angel plaques' which he created for his son Stanley's tomb in Wordsley Churchyard were now safe from vandals and theft at Broadfield House Glass Museum. The general appeal in two local newspapers for donations to cover the cost of replacing the plaques with plain granite panels brought not a single contribution. However, personal approaches to the following resulted in donations which covered the £750 costs:

R. H. Bird (Wordsley Accountant), Black Country Society, Geoff Hill Charitable Trust, Rotary Club of Brierley Hill, Dr. A. Southall (Wordsley Dentist), Wordsley Fish Bar, Wordsley History Society.

**Acknowledgments:**

Broadfield House Glass Museum, Corning Museum of Glass, Johann Van Leerzem, Christopher Perry, John Sanders.

# Working on the Railway—Aged 12!

by Stan Hill

OUR house, one of a terrace of 20, faced the main Worcester to Wolverhampton G.W.R. line 150 yards north of the Brierley Hill railway station. Between the line and the houses was a siding at the end of which was the ' stallage '. This was like a small railway station, with a base, platform high, made of railway sleepers, enclosed on two sides with a G.W.R. station style roof and a small office connected to it. The ' stallage ' stood back from the road, a cul-de-sac, and vans from Marsh & Baxters reversed to the platform and boxes of their sausages consigned to customers in South Wales were unloaded, checked on the platform and loaded into the railway wagon, usually a guard's van in the siding.

This activity was of great interest to the local lads and about half a dozen of us at every opportunity went to ' help ' the porters with the work. I still remember from the age of 10 the names of places in South Wales where our local pig products were destined—Bargoed, Mountain Ash, Abergavenny, Neath, Pontypridd, Briton Ferry.

The arrival and departure of the wagon were interesting events. The former was often from a train arriving at Brierley Hill about 10.30 a.m. from Wolverhampton. A porter went to a points box, hauled the lever over and the Worcester train with ' our ' wagon reversed into the siding until the wagon was at the ' stallage ' platform. The porter then uncoupled it, fixed the vacuum brake, removed the rear lamp and attached it to the end coach and then signalled the all clear to the guard. This led to the green flag being waved and the train resumed its journey.

The picking up of the loaded wagon was by the 4.26 p.m. at Brierley Hill, Wolverhampton to Paddington train. During those early war years, the train was usually pretty full and the unannounced reversing necessary, brought many enquiring faces to the carriage windows.

The coupling up process frightened me. A particular friend amongst the porters, a retired express train driver, re-employed as a porter in 1940, when the young men were called up, used to stand in front of the stationary wagon holding up the coupling chains ready to link up with the last coach of the reversing train as soon as the buffers touched. Occasionally the whole train staggered back a few yards after bumping until the engine driver braked and my friend walked back between the rails and the end two wagons, struggling with the vacuum pipe after successfully dropping the coupling on to the hook of the approaching wagon. I am sure this was forbidden by the rule book.

The ' stallage ' was a marvellous playground and it was only very infrequently that a hostile temporary porter, track ganger or local police-man cleared us off. We could stand on the platform and wave to trains on the main line a few yards away. When the sausage wagon was in the siding we were in and out of that like ants. The most interesting wagon which came were those which contained a proper guards section and were full carriage length.

When the porters had returned to the main station the local lads would be all over the 'stallage' and wagon. Occasionally the cry 'coppers', would be heard and then everyone lay low, those who could, peeping through holes in the wooden walls to watch the Law's progress down West End. Sometimes it was necessary to vacate the whole area when a suspicious policeman climbed over the boundary fence and we escaped along the line, out of view and up into The Bridge Inn's yard, and then to work our way back by a circuitous route to the 'stallage'.

Getting to know the porters at the siding and running errands for them enabled me to work my way into their room at the station and I soon began to spend many hours there from the age of 11. I would assist in any tasks which arose, loading parcels into the guard's van of passenger trains, and collecting tickets and being available to assist passengers with their luggage.

Fish from Fleetwood arrived in one hundredweight boxes for the Central Fish and Chip shop, and I pushed this up the hill on a two-wheeled trolley as soon as it arrived. I always hoped that the proprietor's wife would receive it as she paid me 9 old pence, compared with her husband's 3 old pence. I later found out that the latter thought I had only pushed the box from a van round the corner, and when he saw the vanman later in the week, perhaps he gave him six pence for work about which he new nothing.

Another regular job in the season was to wheel hampers of water cress to the local market. That was a well paid job for an 11 year old, one shilling a time, plus a bunch of cress.

By 1942 I had established myself with all the staff at the station as a useful errand boy, and as one left and was replaced by another I worked my way into the newcomers ' good books '.

My particular friend was J. D. Powell, retired main line express driver, who came back to the railway after the outbreak of war, as a porter on the mid-day shift. By about 1941 he had progressed to leading porter at the age of 62 and worked shifts 6.00 a.m. to 2.00 p.m. one week, 2.00 p.m. to 10.00 p.m. the next. By this time I was at the local grammar school and I frequently went to the station in the evenings and during the long periods between the arrival of trains, there were only about four up and four down during the evening, I did my home-work.

On winter nights we sat in the booking office, which also served as the station master's office. The iron stove near one wall was kept well supplied with coal and with the draught lever out full, the stove pipe was often red hot half way up the ceiling. We must have roasted hundreds of potatoes in the ashes and eaten them with salt not butter, which was in short supply. This was followed by cocoa for me while J.D. popped across to the Railway Inn for half a pint leaving me in

*. . . Struggling with the Vacuum Pipe*          *Drawing: Margaret P. Smith*

On winter nights we sat in the booking office, which also served as the station master's office. The iron stove near one wall was kept well supplied with coal and with the draught lever out full, the stove pipe was often red hot half way up the ceiling. We must have roasted hundreds of potatoes in the ashes and eaten them with salt not butter, which was in short supply. This was followed by cocoa for me while J.D. popped across to the Railway Inn for half a pint leaving me in charge. I kept the door locked and only answered enquiries through the ticket servery.

When trains arrived I'd put on the station master's hat and collect tickets at the exit to the amusement of the regulars. I don't know what supervision there was for no-one ever complained about my presence. It was probably thought that I was the son of one of the porters or the station master.

At the age of 12, I used to look after the station on Sunday nights when old J.D. was on duty. He lived just behind Stourbridge Junction and the last two Sunday trains were 9.29 p.m. on the ' down ' line from Paddington to Wolverhampton and the 10.15 p.m. on the ' up ' line to Stourbridge Junction. He used to board this one and went home leaving me to look after the 9.29 p.m. which was always late—sometimes as much as four hours because of the bombing of London. The guard on this train had worked a train south—probably as far as Worcester and then worked the London train back to Wolverhampton, and J.D., if he knew he was a friendly sort, would tip him off that a substitute would be in charge when he returned—i.e. me at 12 years of age. My father used to pop in on the way home from the Station Inn about 10.30 p.m., but only for a minute or two as he was on duty at 4.30 a.m. next morning at the local post office.

My most frightening experience, I well remember, was when there was a great crowd of relatives seeing a sailor off to his ship. They were merry when they arrived at 9.00 p.m., and were rowdy and boisterous by 1.00 a.m., when the train still hadn't arrived, they raced up and down the dimly lit platform, over the wooden bridge and back again, trundled the heavy four wheeled trolley about and generally enjoyed themselves. I was terrified in case anything or anybody went on the line. Eventually the train arrived, the sailor boarded, his exhausted departure party departed themselves. As the train pulled out I shouted "Goodnight" to the guard who replied "Goodnight Jack", (Jack Powell well asleep by this time). I put out all the gas lamps, one by one, and I nipped along the line, over the fence and through our front door where my mother was still waiting up for me. What responsibility for a 12 year old. But we were never found out and I was glad of the half crown for doing it.

# AN UNUSUAL HOLIDAY

by

Stan Hill

AT the beginning of September many Black Country folk between Wednesbury and Kinver observed a fairly unusual sight for these days. This was two brightly painted small caravans, one drawn by a huge white horse and the other by a smaller chestnut one. Travelling in one van were retired industrial painter Harry Timmins and his wife Margaret and in the other, motor mechanic Brian Saddler, his wife Sue and their son, another Brian, all from Friar Park, Wednesbury.

The Black Country of old was well know for pigeon flying, whippet racing, keeping Staffordshire bull terriers and, before the advent of motor vehicles, horses. The latter, in addition to helping some families to earn their livings, were pets as well.

Harry Timmins's father used and loved horses and his affection for the animals passed down to Harry who has had his present chestnut, Andy, for over 15 years. The Saddlers have had their horse Thunder for over five years. He was bought from a settled Quarry Bank former travelling family and the Saddlers broke him in themselves.

For both families the horses are pets and are used to draw their two-wheeled gigs. This hobby has considerable support in the Tipton/Wednesbury areas. On Sunday mornings when road traffic is lighter as many as 20 to 30 gig outfits make their way to The Golden Cup Inn, an M. & B. house at Tipton, for a gathering. Here, enthusiasts compare equipment, wheel and deal in the accoutrements, compare notes and have a sociable drink before driving home for dinner.

Harry has taken his horse and gig as an attraction to church money raising events, school fetes and at a carnival conveyed the mayor of West Bromwich on one occasion. Wherever they go the horses and gigs arouse much interest, amongst

51

children particularly. Whenever they are out in their locality empty streets soon fill up with inquisitive children. They are fascinated by what earlier this century was commonplace.

The Timminses and the Saddlers have a gipsy friend who calls on them with his family when they are travelling in the Wednesbury area. When the gipsies are on the road in the country the former sometimes visit them. Then they go by car with their towed caravans and share the same camp site. This contact led the Black Country folk to wondering what it would be like to live as gipsies for a period.

They both have their own horses. All they needed were caravans.

Brian had a flat four wheeled cart and adapted that. He fitted caravan springs, used scaffolding poles for axles and fitted four motor car wheels. Then he designed and incorporated a safe braking system using car parts. On the cart he constructed the van using plywood, angle iron and canvas.

Harry bought a small ready made traditional barrel type caravan and spent many hours restoring it.

The two families planned their excursion carefully. First they surveyed the proposed route by car, enquired about the law relating to horse drawn vehicles and noted possible parking sites. They found that, with a horse drawn vehicle it is per-

*In a shady nook between Kinver and Swindon*
*Photograph Geoff Warburton.*

missible to stay on a roadside verge for up to 24 hours. Great care has to be taken not to park in unauthorised places.

The first stage took this unusual group through Tipton, Dudley, Kingswinford, Wall Heath and on to Greensforge. This is 12 miles from home and enough in one day for the horses. They then travelled to Kinver and the third lap took them to Highgate Common. I met them at Greensforge on their way back home.

The travellers were very careful not to leave any traces of having camped overnight. They cooked by calor gas stoves and carried rubbish receptacles on their vans. A friend with a car monitored their progress and when necessary carried the 10 gallons of water the horses need each day – they do two miles to the gallon!

During their brief tour our Black Country holiday makers found that motorists in the countryside were much more tolerant and considerate than those in towns where everybody seems to be in a hurry. Many people en-route have taken notice of them, waved as they drove or stopped and had a chat when they were camped. They have been photographed and videoed and Sue says that everyone has shown great friendliness. For a week they were without newspapers, radio and TV and they did not miss them at all. Their days were full of interest travelling, observing and just living simply. They were lucky with the weather and the experience has set them thinking and already planning a similar holiday in 1994 but for a longer period, perhaps a month, and venturing farther afield. Already Brian is working out a design for another, lighter van, which he will build during the winter months.

Should this account tempt you to think about taking to the open road in a similar manner, remember that the Timminses and the Saddlers have great experience in handling horses, useful skills to meet any vehicle emergencies and they did a lot of preparatory work before embarking on the trip.

As for me, I hope to continue my exploratory trips in 1994, but as during the past 5 years, with Walter Mills Tours, it's easier.

# THE CHRISTMAS FAIR

by

Bert Barr

EIGHT year old Alister William Andrews and his older sister Elizabeth were keen members of their local church where mother was on the Parochial Church Council and father was a sidesman. The annual Church Christmas Fair was an activity to which all the family contributed and preparations began straight after the August holiday.

Every Tuesday morning Mrs. Andrews hosted a soft goods making session when her dinning room was strewn with fabrics, cottons, stuffing materials, tape, patterns and ladies with time to spare. As winter approached huge cardboard television boxes full of saleable items, soft toys, padded coathangers, toilet roll holders, shoe stores and babies' ware accumulated in the spare room.

Mr. Andrews, with other sidesmen, planned to stage a penalty taking competition and a 'smash 'em and bash 'em' stall on the field behind the church hall as their contribution. Elizabeth and her Guides Company had been given the job of running the lucky dips and helping with the refreshments.

Alister's contribution was an individual one. He was given a collecting card and he sought donations from neighbours, relatives and friends whose church attendance was only usually in connection with baptisms, marriages and deaths. As the big day approached his card was nearly full with over £10 subscribed and he felt that he had done his bit. However, his mother was not satisfied. She was never satisfied. On receiving a note from the toy stall organiser she sorted through Alister's toys and found half a dozen seemingly discarded, outgrown items and assembled them on his bed.

"Alister, I've sorted out some of your old toys and put them on your bed. Look them over and see if they can go to the Fair," said Mrs. Andrews when Alister returned from school one day.

When she went upstairs after tea she found that each item had been returned to where she had found it, but she said nothing. Mother went through this procedure twice more with the same result but on the third occasion she was more decisive. After tea there was a cry from the bedroom:

"Mummy, where's my Teddy gone?"

"Alister," replied Mrs. Andrews, "You haven't sent anything to the toy stall. I thought that you have finished with that teddy, it's only got one ear, and one eye, the limbs are loose and it's covered with stains."

Alister said nothing but looked glum for the whole of the evening, and the next day and the day after that. Mrs. Andrews thought he was sickening for something.

The day of the Christmas Fair turned out to be a fine late Autumn day and crowds poured into the church hall. Alister had £1 to spend but was still quiet and glum as he stood with his dad for the opening ceremony.

"Oi 'ev great pleasure in declaring this Christmas Fair open," intoned Miss Harris, the oldest church member who performed the opening ceremony. "Do please spend extravagantly so that the church organ can be repaired." Then there was a rush to the popular stalls.

Alister had reconnoitred the hall and darted off to his objective as soon as Miss Harris had finished. He made his purchase and then joined his father outside on the "smash 'em and bash 'em stall'. This was like a coconut shy but with unglazed ceramic factory discards specially brought in for the event. He put his purchase which was in a plastic bag on the ground while he let off his frustrations on the crockery. Returning to the hall when he had spent all his money his mother remarked that he looked cheerful for the first time in a week.

All the family helped with clearing up and on the return home all gave details of their afternoon's activities, how much their stalls had contributed to the total, what purchases they had made, competitions they had not won, old friends they'd seen. Alister emptied his bag on the table and out fell one-eared Teddy. Mom and Dad exchanged glances but said nothing.

That night when Mrs. Andrews looked in on Alister before retiring herself she could just see in the darkened bedroom the landing light shining on his pillow on which Teddy had resumed his place which he had not occupied for two years.

# The Rector

by
Bert Barr

GRANNY HANDLEY, well over 80, on the death of her husband, came to live next door to us with her widowed daughter and grandchildren, a boy and girl who were playmates of mine, and the lodger.

We children were in and out of each other's homes without formality and whenever I went next door to call for one of my pals, Granny was always sitting in a voluminous black dress, which made me think of Queen Victoria, by the black leaded grate piled high with burning coals.

Granny watched us closely, scarcely ever said anything but she seemed always to be there like a hearth ornament.

One day in early autumn, I remember being surprised by a very talkative Granny, who, when we went through the living room, waved a letter at us.

" He's coming on Christmas Eve. My son Ezra is coming on Christmas Eve. He's a rector you know. Dolly has read me his letter."

Everybody who went to the house, the doctor, milkman, baker, was given the same message. When my mother returned from next door from a regular gossip she was incredulous.

" Granny's son is coming. He's a rector you know." I was very impressed. How could this illiterate old lady have a son a rector? I had been going to church and Sunday School since I was four years old and knew all about rectors, vicars and curates. I was amazed.

As Christmas approached, the impending visit of Granny's son was the talk of the neighbourhood. Where did he live? Where was his church? Did he wear a dog collar? Would he come in a car? — there was only one car — an Austin Ruby, in our and three neighbouring streets.

Proud Granny invited us in to meet her son when he came on Christmas Eve.

" You'll put your Sunday School clothes on when the Rector comes next door ", my mother said.

Granny's excitement grew daily until finally Ezra came. Mother and I went in after tea to meet him. I had been on the look out without success, and he certainly had not come by car.

What a surprise! I had seen a bishop, rectors, vicars, curates, archdeacons, canons, deans and even a prebendary, but I had never seen a rector like Ezra.

Six foot tall, broad shouldered with huge boots, rough cord trousers, a 4 inch wide leather belt around his ample belly, dark shirt and the '30's equivalent of a donkey jacket, he thrust out his hand, with fingers like king-size sausages, at my mother as we went in.

55

THE ' RECTOR '                    Drawn by Glyn Parsons

" 'Ow do, 'ow bin yer? Our ode girl's lookin' well ay 'er? "

It transpired that Ezra was a steel-erector with a local firm with overseas contracts, and had been abroad for two years.

# THE STORM BEFORE THE CALM

by

Bert Barr

GREAT Aunt Amelia had never seen a doctor before I called one when I found her, aged 85, collapsed in her bungalow.

A quick examination and the doctor looked over his half moon spectacles and said, "Dropsy, hospital".

Within an hour Great Aunt was comfortably installed in the local hospital, once a workhouse, the thought of which had previously terrified her. When I visited her that night she seemed perfectly at home. She had been bathed on arrival, wore a nice hospital nightdress and was enjoying the luxury of clean sheets for the first time, as it turned out, for years.

Being the only close relative I visited her every night during that cold January and Great Aunt, contrary to expectations, seemed to accept the situation without complaint. She conversed with other patients' visitors, joined in the community hymn singing on the Sunday evening and when I went into the ward after the Gospel Singers had left she gave me a full account of all that had gone on in that ward during the day.

The next evening I was there early, first in the queue waiting outside the ward for visiting time, 7 p.m. But there was a delay. There was trouble in the ward. Nurses and orderlies wearing harassed looks hurried hither and thither. As the ward doors swung to and fro, with each exit and entrance I could just see that one bed had the screens round. A quarter past seven, half past, quarter to eight passed and then at ten to eight an exhausted looking staff nurse opened the doors and admitted the irritable visitors.

I was first in and made my way quickly down the ward to Great Aunt. She was sitting up, looking quite angelic and serene and smiled as I pulled up a chair.

"What on earth has been going on?" I enquired as I plonked my bag of her requisites and patient's dainties on the bed and pulled up a chair. "I'm freezing. I've been out there over an hour".

"Oh", said Great Aunt, "there has been a palava here tonight. One of the patients has been very troublesome. Oh, she has led the staff a dance. Tell me, how's the weather"?

"Cold and icy, and in the corridor as well", I replied.

"Well, we have had a lovely day today. After a good lunch a group of children came and sang to us and I did enjoy it. At teatime we all had a piece of birthday cake as it is a nurse's birthday today and it was tasty," said Great Aunt.

At 8 p.m., despite our late entrance, the departure bell went on time and I was the last visitor to leave the ward.

On my way past Sister's office she called me. "Mr. Barr", she said, "your great aunt is a very, very difficult patient. Please tell her tomorrow that if we have another performance like that tonight I shall have her transferred to the mental patients' ward."

"But Sister", I replied, "I had no idea . . ."

Next night I was there early as usual but on that occasion there was no delay and

as I strode past Sister's office she called me again. "Mr. Barr, she said, "I am sorry to have to tell you that your Great Aunt died an hour ago."
Sister's request of the previous evening didn't matter any more.

# THE NORTHERN BALLET THEATRE
by
Stan Hill

*Northern Ballet Theatre in 'A Simple Man'*

THE NORTHERN BALLET THEATRE, based in Manchester, is the only top ranking ballet company which vists the Black Country.

The company performed at the Grand Theatre, Wolverhampton, 22 – 25 March 1989 when their programme included 'A Simple Man', based on the life and painting of northern scenes artist L. S. Lowry.

Continuing their policy of selecting the best local children to dance with them on tour the company chose three Black Country children to participate. This year Lisa Caine (10) of Bilston, Rebecca Isherman (10) of Kingswinford and Neil Watkin (11) of Willenhall were chosen and danced superbly.

Northern Ballet, founded in 1969, has Rudolf Nureyev as its artist laureate and Princess Margaret is the company's patron. There are 30 dancers and 30 support staff.

The Arts Council of Great Britain, on whose support Northern Ballet depends, commissioned an investigation into the future of dance and this resulted in the Devlin Report, published in January 1989 which recommended that the Manchester company's subsidy be ended. Northern Ballet refused to performances by the company were impressed by the curtain speech of Christopher Gable (artistic director) at Wolverhampton when he appealed for support against the threat. The Committee discussed the matter and the following resolution, together with a statement about the strength of the Black Country Society, was forwarded to the Arts Council before its crucial 26 April 1989 meeting:

> *"The Black Country Society deplores the Devlin Report's recommendation that the grant to the Northern Ballet Theatre be withdrawn, and strongly urges the Arts Council to continue to give the financial support necessary to enable this superb company to continue and develop. The Arts in the Black Country and the West Midlands generally would be poorer without their eagerly awaited visits".*

Our resolution supplemented more than 12,000 individual protest communications to the Arts Council.

Mr. Luke Rittner, Secretary-General of the Arts Council later announced that the Manchester company's grant will be safe for the next two years.

Black Country folk should look out for Northern Ballet's next visit and go and see them to enjoy the sort of magnificent theatrical experience normally only regularly available in London.

# BLACK COUNTRY PUBLIC ART SCULPTURES

## 'JOHN NORTHWOOD AND THE PORTLAND VASE'

JOHN Northwood, born in 1836 at Wordsley, was put to work at the Wordsley glassworks of Messrs. W.H.B. and J. Richardson where his talent for drawing was noticed and encouraged. After some time the works closed temporarily and John joined his older brother William, a builder, and helped to build houses in the Wordsley area. When the works reopened under Mr. B. Richardson John re-entered the glass trade and was influenced by skilled artists and craftsmen such as Thomas Bott, the brothers Muckley, J. Locke, Phillip Pargeter, E. Guest and others.

It was while working at Richardsons that John Northwood heard of the renowned piece of Roman cameo glass, 'The Portland Vase'. In 1845, in the Hamilton Gallery of the British Museum, the vase was smashed into about 200 fragments by a vandal. It was skilfully repaired in 1845, again in 1947 and more recently in 1989.

*Sculptor Anthony Stones holding a model of his sculpture of John Northwood with his replica of The Portland Vase.*

*Photograph by courtesy of Chelsfield plc.*

It was during his resumed glass career that Northwood heard his employer ("Uncle Ben", he called him) state, "Anyone who reproduced that vase faithfully in glass could command £1,000 for it", and he never forgot it.

From 1860, Northwood, by that time a skilled decorator, was in partnership with his younger brother and two others in a glass decorating business near Barnett Lane, Wordsley. After a year it became J. and J. Northwood (John and Joseph). After 9 years spare time work, John completed the 'Elgin' Vase for Sir Benjamin Stone who later presented it to Birmingham Art Gallery. This practical experience, where the sculptor had to devise his own tools and methods for the delicate carving was the background which gave him the confidence to take up his cousin Phillip Pargeter's challenge to produce a glass reproduction of The Portland Vase. Eventually, in 1873, Daniel Hancock, a glassblower at Pargeter's Red House Glassworks and ancestor of a former Mayoress of Dudley, Mrs. J. Simpson, produced an accurate blank and Northwood commenced work on it.

After three years, in 1876 the lost art of glass decoration which had flourished in Roman times but had been lost for nearly 2,000 years, was reborn.

It is fitting that Chelsfield plc, owners of the Merry Hill Centre, should commemorate this famous Black Country man with a full size, open air sculpture, just a few hundred yards from the famous Stevens and Williams Glassworks, where John

Northwood had been Works Manager and Art Director.

The sculptor, Anthony Stones, gained his grounding at the Manchester Regional College of Art. He is a Fellow Member of the Royal Society of British Sculptors and the Royal Society of Arts. In addition he is President of the Society of Portrait Sculptors. He is an accomplished sculptor in his chosen medium of bronze and has his work on display across the globe. Amongst Anthony's sculptures on display in the UK are 'Captain Cook' at the National Maritime Museum, Greenwich; 'Victorian Navvy' at Gerrard's Cross Railway Station; 'Bonnie Prince Charlie' at Manchester Piccadilly Railway Station.

*Compiled by the Editor using "John Northwood - His Contribution to the Stourbridge Flint Glass Industry, 1850-1902", by John Northwood II, Pub. Mark & Moody, 1958; "The Breaking and Remaking of The Portland Vase", by Nigel Williams, pub. British Museum Publications, 1989; and material from Chelsfield plc.*

# SURVIVOR UNVEILS PLAQUE TO
# BLACK COUNTRY AUTHOR

Halesowen born author Dr. Francis Brett Young practised in Brixham for several years from 1907. When he took a partner he left his original premises and with his wife moved to The Old Garden House, Berry Head.

On 29th April 1994 a plaque was unveiled on The Old Garden House to mark the author's occupancy of it. Mrs. Elsie Stabb, now in her eighties, performed the unveiling ceremony. She was asked to officiate for a very interesting reason. Dr. Francis Brett Young was called to her when, as a two year old, she was near death. He diagnosed diphtheria and double pneumonia. He should have sent her to Torquay Isolation Hospital but knew that she would not survive the journey. Instead she was rushed to Brixham Cottage Hospital. Dr. Brett Young performed a tracheotomy to enable her to breathe properly. Elsie survived and has since lived a very active life in Brixham.

The novelist used the life saving incident in 'My Brother Jonathan', set in Wednesford', which was made into a film in 1948 with Michael Denison and Dulcie Gray. This had been shown on television several times.

Alan Rankin, Editor of the FBY Journal and founder member of the Francis Brett Young Society which paid for the plaque, attended the unveiling and read extracts from 'Deep Sea' set in Brixham.

*Acknowledgments: Pat Nicholls, Alan Rankin, Valda Sheldon.*

# Unveiling of the Tipton Slasher Statue

O N Spring Bank Holiday Monday, May 3rd 1993, at 11 a.m. over 1,000 people gathered in Coronation Gardens, Tipton, to witness the unveiling of the Tipton Slasher Statue by His Worship The Mayor of Sandwell, Councillor John Sullivan. This was the culmination of just a few months sustained effort by a group of local folk led by Jim Holland (Chairman), Councillor Brett Bates (Secretary), Chris Martin (Treasurer) and Martin Collinson (Marketing) supported by consultants John Brimble J.P., Keith Hodgkins and Ian Walden OBE who were determined to commemorate Tipton's most famous son, William Perry (1819-1880) Champion of England Bare Knuckle Boxing (1850-1857).

The life size bronze statue was designed by Tipton silversmith and sculptor, Bill Haynes and is a striking piece of public art.

Fund raising only started in October 1992 and for the organisers to have been able to arrange the unveiling only seven months later demonstrates Black Country determination on the part of the Committee reminiscent of the great days of entrepreneurial spirit when the Slasher was Champion.

There is still some way to go and the appeal for donations continues. In addition a limited number of 12" bronze statues is still available at £250.

On Unveiling Day celebrations continued until dusk with contributions by several groups and throughout the afternoon there were free canal boat trips from Coronation Gardens to the Marina in Sandwell and back. The events concluded with a grand fireworks display witnessed by about 800 spectators.

It was a great day for Tipton.

# BLACK COUNTRY AIR RAID ALERTS AND INCIDENTS

THE reference in the feature on Len Pardoe in the winter issue had brought forward more information about air raid alerts and incidents during the last war.

Graham Beckley, member of the Black Country Society Committee had an interesting memento of the landmines which fell on Quarry Bank in 1940. Graham's grandfather, Ebby Beckley, of Beckley's Garage, Brierley Hill, had been a volunteer fireman at Brierley Hill for many years and attended the Quarry Bank incident on 20th December 1940. The landmines were defused and Captain Beckley acquired the nosecone of one of them and took it back to the garage. Here, after the war it was made into a child's pedal car for Graham, by his father Bob, Ebby's son. His daughter Joan still uses a length of a landmine's parachute cord as a dressing gown belt.

In the Brierley Hill area and the parishes of Kinver, Enville, Bobbington and Himley there were some 358 air raid alerts until the end of 1944. Some 72 high explosive bombs, an oil bomb and over 200 incendiaries fell on the area. Two bombers crashed and there was slight damage from drifting barrage balloons.

The worst damage from enemy action was in Fisher Street, Brierley Hill where 2 houses were demolished. There were no fatalities from the air raids.

The only fatality within the district occurred on 16th April 1944 when a heavy bomber returning from a 1,000 bomber raid on Stuttgart crashed in Adelaide Street, Brierley Hill. Major damage was caused to 7 houses and there was a fatality. A young married woman, Mrs. Bessie Rowbottom, aged 32, whose husband was in the R.A.F., that night stayed at her parents' Adelaide Street home, after visiting the cinema at Brierley Hill and died in the crash. About 60 houses needed repairs, some a quarter of a mile away.

All of the crew bailed out safely and made their way to Brierley Hill Police Station.

*Acknowledgments: Graham Beckley, Jack Genner, David Newton (an Adelaide Street survivor).*

*Graham Beckley in his special pedal car.*

# THE FOOLISH PEOPLE

The eight-fifteen to Paradise
    Begins at Blowers Green
And whisks you down to Severn's banks
    By many a sylvan scene
To Bewdley, Highley, Hampton Loade,
    And all the vales between.

The eight-fifteen to Paradise
    Proceeds by Holly Hall
From which you get to Abberley
    With no delay at all,
And Hopton Wafers, Rock and Teme
    Are at your beck and call.

The eight-fifteen to Paradise
    Stops next at Brierley Hill,
And so to Clent and Clee and Clun
    And whereo'er you will:
To spots like Wyre or Wenlock Edge
    Where men may gaze their fill.

But ah! the dolts of Blowers Green
    Neglect this magic train;
At Holly Hall, at Brierley Hill,
    In torpor they remain:
Alone I go to Paradise
    And I do not complain.

*Editor's comment: I think that the poet was unfairly critical of the inhabitants of Blowers Green, Holly Hall and Brierley Hill whom he alleged neglected 'this magic train'. They might have neglected the one on which he travelled and for very good reason, but they did not neglect the line. In the 1930s and war-time they worked 6 days a week, when work was available, but in Spring, Summer and Autumn the trains from the Black Country to the Severn Valley were packed on Sundays.*

*Frequently our family joined an early morning Sunday Worcester train at Brierley Hill changing at Stourbridge Junction to catch the Snow Hill-Bridgnorth train, which having stopped at several Black Country stations on the way down was usually packed, and we stood in the corridor until some passengers alighted at Bewdley. We continued, perhaps to Eardington and during the day would walk back along the river bank to Highley to return from there in the evening. Glorious days! Bewdley was our Benidorm and Arley our Alicante!*

*The poet must have made his excursions when everybody else was at work. He could easily have done this as he was a schoolmaster with long holidays.*

*From* The Lady *February 7th 2005*

# The Changing Face of The Black Country

One of the earliest uses of the term "the Black Country" can be found in *Rides on Railways* by Samuel Sidney, published in 1851. Chapter Two of Walter White's *All Around the Wrekin* (1860) has the phrase as its title. But it is probably best-known when used in the title of Elihu Burritt's *Walks in the Black Country and Its Green Borderland* (1868). Some of these writers refer to the phrase as a local term, so it is likely it was coined within the district, itself, in the 1830s and 1840s.

The Black Country relates to an area of some 150 square miles north-west of Birmingham (but excluding that city), wherein lay a coal seam that was nearly 33 feet deep and was known locally as The Thick.

Outcrops of coal had been discovered in the 13th century and were extracted by simple opencast methods, followed by bell pits and, from the mid-18th century, pits of a style more familiar to us today.

The increase in the amount of coal produced in the 17th century coincided with royal edicts forbidding the use of timber as a fuel for the furnaces and kilns of the emerging industries – their demands were consuming the forests, thus threatening the building of ships.

For hundreds of years, iron-smelters had used wood in the form of charcoal as a fuel. This method took five tons of wood to produce one ton of charcoal. Britain's ancient forests were being destroyed – and her security was at risk.

The use of coal instead of charcoal in the smelting of iron ore is attributed to Dudley-born Abraham Darby in 1709, when working in Coalbrookdale. This was really the start of the Industrial Revolution. As the door was closing on wood as a fuel, another opened with coal, which became available in increasing quantities just at the right time.

At first, water in the mines limited the depth to which pits could be sunk. Then, Thomas Newcomen developed a pumping-engine and one was installed a mile from Dudley Castle at Tipton, in 1712. These became widespread in the area and allowed coal production to increase considerably as deeper pits could be sunk and kept relatively dry.

At the same time other minerals were found in abundance: iron ore, clay and limestone, an essential ingredient for the iron-smelting process. All of these materials were soon extensively mined, or quarried, throughout the area as the Industrial Revolution gathered pace. These reserves in the south of the Black Country had also attracted immigrant glassmakers during the 1600s.

Nevertheless, before 1750, the Black Country was predominantly rural and most of its inhabitants enjoyed a mainly agricultural lifestyle – until huge changes were brought about by the 18th-century Enclosure Acts. Small industries were craftsmen-orientated and the original power sources were human, or wind and water. The growth of industry was made possible by the discovery of minerals and the invention of steam-engines, mechanised processes, the vast expansion of the iron industry and the building of canals and railways. Yet, even during this period of intense industrial change, there was still a rural look to the landscape, particularly in areas where coal near the surface had

65

been exhausted and the despoiled land had reverted to nature.

During this 150-year transformation the people formed closely knit communities largely through the hardships that they experienced. Families were large, infant mortality high, life expectancy low and there was a local feeling of being different from others. Customs and language peculiar to the coalfield developed and, despite modern media influences, they have remained strong.

Within the space of 60 years two major developments in the world of transport – the canals and the railway – greatly facilitated the expansion of local coal and iron industries. Canals used much iron in their mechanisms and could transport coal and iron in huge quantities. Railways followed suit and both systems used and fed industry's growing demands.

From the early 18th century there was an influx of country folk from the surrounding counties into the area. Housing settlements developed around pits and ironworks. Hovels were thrown up to accommodate these newcomers and their families and, gradually, without any planning, industrial hamlets grew up in the formerly rural landscape.

After lasting for a century, many of these industrial hamlets withered away once the easily accessible coal had been exhausted. Other hamlets grew up and joined neighbouring settlements, perhaps to become an industrial village. Some of them became small industrial towns and developed their own specialities – for example, Wednesbury (iron and steel, heavy railway equipment, tubes), Bilston (iron and steel), Brierley Hill (iron and steel, maritime safety equipment, crystal glass), Cradley Heath (chains), The Lye (horseshoes, galvanised ware), Walsall (leather), Wolverhampton (galvanised corrugated iron, locomotives), Tipton (iron and steel), Stourbridge (crystal glass, iron rolling), West Bromwich (constructional engineering). While, throughout the Black Country, smaller industrial specialist firms formed to produce the iron and steel products needed by a growing economy. By 1860 the Black Country had reached its peak of industrial production.

The uncontrolled, uncoordinated and unplanned industrialisation continued. As industry expanded, the sub-region acted like a sponge, absorbing incomers who were hastily accommodated in what were to become slums – for these were the days when there was no fresh water supply, sewage disposal, paved roads, street lighting or refuse collection.

In the 19th century most of industry was powered by coal. Most houses depended upon it for heating, cooking and lighting (gas for lighting came from coal). The smoke produced was like a thick black fog over the district.

After passing through the district in 1803, Robert Southey (later to become Poet Laureate) wrote:

"Everywhere the tower of some manufacturing was to be seen in the distance, vomiting up flames with smoke and blasting everything around with metallic vapours."

Unfortunately its civil administration was not equipped to deal with the changing situation. Ancient manorial courts and parochial church councils continued to try and deal with some of the problems, while older towns obtained Charters of Incorporation achieving some local control. There followed Improvement Acts, local Boards of Health and of Education in an attempt to alleviate the bad effects of industrialisation.

A major step forward in civil administration came in 1888 with the creation of County Councils, which gradually absorbed the functions of old established and ad-hoc bodies. Counties were subdivided into districts in 1894. By this time, in the Black Country, there were 23 areas of joined-up industrial townships which were granted their own local councils. Since then there has been a succession of reorganisations that, in 1974, created four Metropolitan Boroughs – Dudley, Sandwell, Wolverhampton and Walsall – between them absorbing all of the other local council areas of the Black Country and two adjoining ones. But the actual boundaries of "The Black Country" were never clear cut. This 19th-century term was used locally and quite loosely to describe the area. Now, however, the four boroughs mentioned are designated Black Country Metropolitan Boroughs, so after 180 years the nickname is officially accepted.

Over the past 150 years, successive bodies, both national and local, have striven to rectify the damage caused by industrialisation and they have been so successful that visitors coming to the area for the first time have suggested the area be renamed "The Green Country".

# MAYORS HONOUR MEMORY OF MIDLANDS AUTHOR

by
Stan Hill

HALESOWEN Parish Church was the setting for a civic service to commemorate the 50th anniversary of the death of Midlands poet and novelist Francis Brett Young (1884-1954). The 300+ congregation, led by the civic heads of Birmingham, Coventry, Wolverhampton, Dudley, Sandwell, Solihull, Walsall and North Warwickshire, Sylvia Heal, M.P., Deputy Speaker of the House of Commons and invited guests, watched as the Mayor of Dudley, Councillor Rosemary Tomkinson, laid a wreath at the Brett Young memorial and heard a reading from Young's novel, *Wistanslow*, describing worship in Halesowen Church.

Brett Young, the Midlands' most prolific regional novelist, used Birmingham, the Black Country and their surroundings as the setting for his plots. No less than twenty-five out of his thirty novels feature 'North Bromwich' - his name for Birmingham.

The Rector of Halesowen, Canon John Everest, conducted the service; the Bishop of Dudley, Rt. Rev. David Walker, led prayers and Michael Hall, Chairman of the Francis Brett Young Society, gave the address.

67

To mark this anniversary year, Royal Worcester Porcelain has produced a limited edition commemorative plate to a design by Hagley artist Alan Pritchard. As a memento of the service, the Francis Brett Young Society presented plates (depicting Halesowen Church, where Young was baptised, Worcester Cathedral, where his ashes are interred and Chaddesley Corbett, typical of his many Worcestershire settings) to each of the civic heads attending.

The service was one of over fifty events arranged this year by the Francis Brett Young Society to celebrate Brett Young's life and works.

*The Mayor of Dudley, Councillor Rosemary Tomkinson, laying the wreath at the Francis Brett Young memorial, after the service.*

*Left to Right: Linda Button (Membership Secretary), Martyn Round (Committee Member), Stan Hill (Past President), Mrs Barbara Julian, Miss Joan White (President) and Mr Ron Julian (Past President).*

# 4.

# A selection of
# book reviews

As well as charting the variety of books *The Blackcountryman* receives for review, and a flavour of
launch parties an Editor is invited to, this chapter celebrates Stan's admiration for the Halesowen
novelist Francis Brett Young (1884-1954), and how
he forged a link with Sutton Publishing in their
'Britain in Old Photographs' series. This encouraged
many local authors to participate in that Company's
publishing programme.

## BOOK REVIEW: A G.P.'s Progress to the Black Country

*' A G.P.'s Progress to the Black Country ' by Francis Maylett Smith.
Edited by Denis Hayes Crofton, Volturna Press, 151 pp. Available from
D. H. Crofton, 26 Vauxhall Gardens, Tonbridge, Kent, at £5.90 (inc.
p. & p.).*

FRANCIS MAYLETT SMITH was a popular doctor in Quarry Bank
from 1916 until he retired in 1933. He is affectionately remembered
by elderly Quarry Bankers, and those to whom I have mentioned him
referred to his ear trumpet, bicycle and car.

Dr. Smith's developing deafness caused him to abandon his medical
training at St. Mary's Hospital and to enter an agricultural college near
Cape Town. Here however, in the absence of qualified doctors he
practiced amongst his fellow students and natives. This renewed his interest
in medicine and despite his hearing handicap, after eight more months'

in medicine and despite his hearing handicap, after eight more months' study at Steeven's Hospital, Dublin, returned to London for his finals and qualified as a doctor at the age of 30.

After a year's locum work, Dr. Smith worked for eight years in South Wales (see ' Surgery at Aberffrwd ', Volturna Press) and then had saved enough to buy the practice at Quarry Bank, referred to throughout the text as Collier's Forge.

The first half of the book covers the doctor's experiences searching for jobs and his eager acceptance of short-term locum positions. One prospective employer, on learning that two of his patients had died during a short-term locum engagement, remarked, " You have some practice in signing death certificates, at any rate! " Eventually he went to South Wales and after a brief undemanding job in Southampton bought the Black Country practice.

The second half of the book describes a doctor's work in a poor Black Country working class industrial township from the middle of the First World War until the early thirties. The disguised place names are easily identifiable.

Dr. Smith's account of his work in Quarry Bank is a fascinating record of health care 30 years before the National Health Service. He battled valiently against a measles epidemic in 1917 and waves of influenza in 1918, finally succumbing himself after three weeks and developing pneumonia.

The effects of the war on the locality are described and his accounts of the Zeppelin raids confirm what I heard about them from my own Quarry Bank relatives 50 years ago.

The new post-war vicar's attack on religious apathy is entertaining and it is interesting to note that one at least of his innovations still continues in present parish affairs. The doctor however was a passive but cash contributing observer in all of the new activities.

Dr. Smith retired to Church Stretton in 1933, then to Sussex, returning to Shropshire during the Second World War to help a local doctor, and died there in 1945 aged 67.

The Editor, Denis Hayes Crofton, Dr. Smith's nephew, by publishing the accounts, has contributed greatly to our knowledge of the social and economic conditions of a small Black Country township of 70 years ago and to the history of medical practice.

The dust cover, taken from a water colour painted by the Editor about 60 years ago, of the view from the doctor's house, is worth close scrutiny and comparison with the view today. It shows clearly Homer Hill with pit-head gear, factories in the Stour Valley, Netherend Unitarian Church in the middle distance and Clent beyond.

This is a most enjoyable book, the author of which obviously had an acutely sensitive eye and clear memory despite, or perhaps because of, his deafness, and his sense of humour is apparent throughout.

# BOOK REVIEW: Classroom Museums

*'Classroom Museums' by Dr. John West. 340 pp 8" x 6", 100+ illustrations, published by and available from Elm Publications, 12 Blackstone Road, Huntingdon, Cambs. PE18 6EF price £7.95p.*

NON-TEACHERS, do not be distracted by the title – please read on. This book is another comprehensive aid for teachers of History from the prolific pen (computer actually) of Black Country Society member and 'Blackcountryman' contributor, Dr. John West, for many years one of the country's leading figures in the field of research into History Teaching and author of such standard general works as 'Village Records' (MacMillan 1962, Phillimore 1982) and 'Town Records' (Phillimore 1983). But the book could have as a sub-title 'Collectors and history enthusiasts – get your personal collections better organised and extend them', for the volume will be of consuming interest to all who read this magazine, teachers or not.

The book is a direct response to the Final Report (April 1990) of the History Working Group for the National Curriculum and the fact that included in this Final Report are recommendations on the lines of the author's work over many years based on his extensive doctoral research must be very gratifying to him. This volume outlines an approach to accommodate some of the recommendations, to great advantage.

Chapter One gives a resume 'Museums Today' and lists by themes those most likely to be useful, nationwide.

'Starting a Collection', Chapter Two, gives plenty of ideas and with a hundred objects illustrated and analysed in Chapter Three the new collector will soon be 'on his way'. Here you can discover where to buy Civil War Balls at 50p each, early documents from the 16th century from £6 each, Roman items from £2, medieval thimbles for £1 – £20 and hundreds of other items, original and reproduction.

Peruse the 200 pages on the 'objects' and you will soon be searching your attics for discarded items, which given the author's treatment will provide Society members, their children and/or grandchildren much interest.

I have already completed a card on the lines suggested for a new acquisition in my own collection, an oil lamp from the Wall Heath level crossing gates of the former Pensnett Railway.

For teachers this guide will be invaluable.

# BOOK REVIEW: The Loaded Hour - a History of the Express and Star

*'The Loaded Hour – a History of the Express & Star' by Peter Rhodes, 252 pp, A5 flexibound £4.99p, Hardback £15, from Star Shops, Express & Star offices or by post, (extra £2.50).*

This is an up-to-date account of the development of a small town newspaper from its modest beginnings to the present position as the largest selling regional newspaper in Britain.

The story starts with reference to a casual meeting in the 1860s between Thomas Graham, a Wolverhampton butcher and multi-millionaire industrialist, Andrew Carnegie, both of whom originated from Dunfermline. A friendship developed which resulted in Carnegie financing the purchase of the 'liberal' Evening Star in 1882. He saw the step as a move in the direction of revolution. Graham, who became Carnegie's Wolverhampton general manager, had less radical ambitions. Two years later the 'conservative' Evening Express was absorbed. Eventually Carnegie pulled out and Graham gained full control, probably the key factor in this amazing success story, for the Graham family has been in control ever since, all following policies which have led to a continuous strengthening and expansion of the business from Wolverhampton outwards.

But this is not a dry company history. It is a lively account, peppered with interesting anecdotes and background information: Thomas Graham and Carnegie's friendship, the Canadian experiences which greatly influenced Malcolm Graham, Thomas's grandson, Malcolm's approach to the business, the Wolverhampton built Sunbeam Golden Arrow and Sir Henry Seigrave, what the Prince of Wales did immediately before he opened the Birmingham New Road in 1927, how Star Shops division came to be set up, Leslie Stallard's head, to name a few, and many scoops and exclusives from home and abroad. In fact, the book incorporates a history of national and international events and the Express & Star's reaction to them.

These general matters make very interesting reading but the key to this newspaper's pre-eminence in the press field is clear: throughout its history, advances on a broad front: up-dating equipment, staff training and enlightened staff management, services to the public, development of library facilities, property acquisitions and then on top of this rock solid base built up over the years the application before any other British newspaper of the most modern technology to news gathering and printing. The opposition hadn't a chance. All of this has come about because of the consistent management policy of ploughing back into the business a high percentage of profits each year. If only British industry had done this Governments would not now be in the position of "Keep rearranging the deck chairs on the 'Titanic' ".

No wonder the Express & Star is known as 'the Black Country Bible'! Peter Rhodes, the newspaper's Chief Feature Writer and Press Awards winner has produced a book which every students of the Black Country, at whatever level, should have.

***The Rare and the Beautiful - the Lives of the Garmans*** by Cressida
Connolly, published by Fourth Estate, ISBN 1-84115-633-7, price £16.99

Dr Walter Garman was Medical Officer of Health for Wednesbury from 1888, and had a
medical practice which he conducted from the family home, Oakswell Hall, Wednesbury.
By 1911, he and his wife Marjorie had produced nine children: seven girls and two boys.
This book describes in detail the amazing lives of three of the sisters, who were 'let loose'
(or perhaps 'escaped') to London immediately after World War I. Mary married left-wing
South African poet, Roy Campbell (though that did not restrain her), Kathleen became the
model and mistress of Jacob Epstein, sculptor, artist and art collector, and Lorna had
affairs with Laurie Lee and bore him a daughter, and artist Lucien Freud. Lee and Freud
both later married nieces of Lorna.

The end of the book gives the explanation as to how the Black Country comes to have a
most magnificent art collection; eventually sometime after Epstein had become a widower
he married Kathleen and when he was knighted, she became Lady Epstein. She inherited
Epstein's collection and donated a considerable part of it (the Garman Ryan Collection) to
Walsall, near where she was raised.

# BOOK REVIEW: The Black Country Year Book and Who's Who, 1993-4

*'The Black Country Year Book and Who's Who, 1993-4' published by Kingslea
Press Ltd., Birmingham, Price £18.90 + £2.80 p&p.*

Produced by the publishers of the well known 'Birmingham Post & Mail Year
Book and Who's Who' and sponsored by the Black Country Development
Corporation, this first ever 'Black Country Year Book and Who's Who, 1993-4' is a
mine of information about the Black Country. It covers the four Black Country
Boroughs and includes details of Councils' and Government departments, Trade,
Commercial, Industrial, and Professional lists and 25 additional sections from
Banks to Voluntary Organisations, in the latter of which the Black Country Society
is well represented.

The 'Who's Who' section includes over 500 personal entries from which I have
so far identified 15 members of the Black Country Society.

This is an essential reference book for all who have any business or leisure interest in the Black Country and it must be the final nail in the coffin of that daft idea
by a former 'quango' chairman that the name 'The Black Country' should be
dropped.                                                                    S.H.

# BOOK REVIEW: Pat Collins - King of Showmen

*'Pat Collins – King of Showmen' by Freda Allen and Ned Williams, 266pp A4 Hardback, inch. 251 b & w and 8 colour photographs, 38 reproductions of advertisements, handbills, newspaper cuttings etc. Pub. Uralia Press, 23 Westland Road, Wolverhampton W33 9NZ. Price £15 plus £3.25 p & p.*

The idea for this book originated during intervals at Black Country Society Committee meetings when two members, Freda Allen and Ned Williams got to talking about their interest in Pat Collins, Freda from her project on the Bloxwich showman which she had undertaken for her 1988 degree at Wolverhampton Polytechnic, Ned because of Pat Collins's early interest in film showing about which he had written an article in 'The Blackcountryman' Vol. 19. No. 3.

This is an amazing book about an amazing character who arrived in Walsall with his wife in a pony drawn van and children's ride in 1882, almost penniless, and rested at Birchills. From this rock bottom start he proceeded to become a very successful businessman, benefactor, Walsall Town Councillor, Liberal Member of Parliament for Walsall, Alderman, Freeman and Mayor of Walsall.

By 1900 Pat Collins had built up four travelling fairs on sites for which he had the rights, gradually buying many of them; he was always on the lookout for new thrills to offer to the public and always had the best equipment. From then on the story is one of overall continuous progress despite setbacks, wars, miners' strikes and recessions. The fair's attractions bring back memories: Dodgems, Steam Yachts, Watzers, Gallopers, Caterpillars, Cake Walk, Octopus, Flying Flees, Ghost Train, Loop o' Planes, Wall of Death, to name a few. Pat acquired cinemas, theatres, skating rinks and amusement parks and was President of the Showmen's Guild from 1909 to 1929. A lively Member of Parliament, he was able to influence legislation relating to giving them a better image.

Pat's life and interests and the Collins' dynasty and individual members' involvement in the business are extensively detailed in the first half of the book. The second half gives a wide ranging coverage of the business of running travelling fairs and static amusement parks. The section on Fairground Transport (Burrells, Fosters, McLarens, Scammels, Fodens) includes 44 photographs and details of these road giants. The extensive Who's Who and Personal Testimonies in the Appendices complete a fascinating book.

This is a great handbook for devotees of fairs, fairground rides, fairground organs, haulage vehicles, modellers as well as for Black Country folk who'd like to know more about this Black Country man by adoption, and his family who helped to build the business which travelled as far as Hull, York and Nottingham.

Our two researchers/authors did much interviewing and travelling over a period of three years to obtain all the information and their general investigative success with people noted for their reluctance to talk about themselves and associates indicates that they would have become top detectives had they chosen police careers.

Nowhere is the saying that behind every successful man is a powerful woman more apt than in this branch of show business. This was certainly so with Pat Collins whose first wife of 53 years marriage, Flora was a great support, as was Clara whom he married after Flora's death. After Pat's death, Clara, with other trustees, ran the business. Other principals in the business all had wives who took their turn on the machines when necessary.

Imaginative teachers will find in this biography leads to excite and motivate pupils in class projects for weeks.

To launch the book a charity model funfair exhibition was held at St. Patrick's School, Walsall on 23rd November last. Hundreds attended and donations were made to Walsall's Rainbow Hospice and St. Patrick's School. Over 700 books were sold on the day, many being signed by two of Pat's grandchildren, Pat Collins of Barry Island and Vanessa of Lichfield, as well as the authors.

Hurry to get your order in while there are still some books left – it will soon be commanding 'over the odds' at bookfairs, as is Ned's 'Cinemas of The Black Country'.

## BOOK REVIEW: Epstein

*'Epstein' by Stephen Gardiner, pub. by Flamingo, £8.95p. 532 pp, 40 b/w photographs.*

Black Country interest in Sir Jacob Epstein arises partly because one of his models from 1920 was Kathleen Garman, daughter of wealthy Wednesbury Dr. Walter Challinor Garman of Oakeswell Hall.

This monumental work records Epstein's early struggles, his battles with the artistic establishment and his relationships. His first wife died in 1947 after which the remarkable Kathleen brought order into his chaotic household. He married her in 1955. Lady Epstein donated the Garman-Ryan Collection to Walsall in 1972 and Black Country folk can enjoy this amazing personal collection which includes such famous Epstein pieces as Madonna and Child, Meum, Baby Awake, the first Kathleen and Esther, a Constable, Renoir, Modigliani, Van Goh, 3 Corots and many other works by notable painters.

How fortunate for us that Kathleen remembered her Black Country roots when she was dispersing Epstein's vast collection.                                    S.H.

# BOOK REVIEW: Life in Britain since 1930

'*Life in Britain since 1930*' *(Timespan Series TELLTALE 5) by John West, pub. ELM Publications, Seaton House, Kings Ripton, Huntingdon PE17 2NJ. 270pp price £8.95p.*

'Britain since 1930' is a Core study unit for Key Stage 2 in the new compulsory National Curriculum (History). Here is another most valuable book for teachers covering the prescribed period. The approach is that developed by the author as a result of his massive doctoral research project into how children learn about the past ('Children's Awareness of the Past' – (C.A.P.) – 1974–1981), some of the findings of which have been incorporated in the National Curriculum recommendations.

There are 21 story subjects ranging from 'Amy Johnson-Aviator' to 'Very Young Soldiers', some of which have a variety of extracts, 'Ordinary People' for example has 11 accounts. Then follows 'The Evidence' and suggestions how to check it, background information on each of the accounts and 'What is Your Verdict?' which can be as intense as the teacher wishes. This section helps children to relate and compare their own experiences with the subject. The extracts include newspaper stories, popular songs and rhymes, film and radio references, a Royal broadcast, personal reminiscences and diaries, oral evidence, official records and autobiography.

The Appendices cover 'Criteria for Checking Evidence', Criteria for 'Verdict' questions, a Glossary and details of other publications in the 'Timespan' series with related items which will enhance the application of the scheme in the classroom: 'Classroom Museum', 'Classroom Gallery' and 'Classroom Archives'. There is also a folder of 32 support pictures. These are mainly newspaper items, documents, scenes from the film 'The Private Life of Henry VIII', an aircraft identification chart and the sheet music and words for 'Amy, Wonderful Amy' published at the time.

## NON-TEACHERS (and teachers) PLEASE READ ON:

This book will be of great interest to all Black Country Society members because the period of the action of the accounts is that of their lifetime, 1930-74+, which is already history for the children using the book.

Relive the excitement of the news of Amy Johnson's solo flight to Australia, the controversy of 'Bodyline' bowling and the Abdication, the miracles of Dunkirk and the Battle of Britain and a dozen or so other events of the period.

The Black Country Society will be gratified to learn of this leading Education author's approval of 'The Blackcountryman' for he has selected a dozen contributions from back issues for the 'Ordinary Folk' section (32 pages), all of the contributors to which are Black Country folk. The Society and the magazine receive excellent coverage in the book which will be used nationwide. The author states that founder and Editor of the first 83 issues, Harold Parsons, had a great influence on the development of local studies in the Black Country.

The background information to each section will help many members to see some of the events they have lived through in a new light.

No teacher of History in the primary school should be without access to this book and adults in general will find it fascinating.

Any member wishing to purchase a copy should contact the Editor.

# Book Reviews:

***Published Works of Francis Brett Young*** - A Bibliography by Michael Hall, 154 A4pp, s/b/, 41 b/w illustrations, published by The Francis Brett Young Society at £9.95p plus £" p & p.

The Black Country's best known author (1884 - 1954) had 45 major novels published, and his other writings included short stories, poems and articles for newspapers and magazines. In this exhaustive work, Michael Hall, already a biographer of Francis Brett Young has assembled details of the whole range of the author's literary output over more than 50 years. This volume includes a brief synopsis of each of thirty of the novels, and, in most cases, details of publishers, foreign translations, prefaces, dedications, including two to Prime Ministers, and the earliest known review. Similar treatment is applied to his anthologies and works of non-fiction. There is coverage of the author's poetry, including an analysis of his epic poem 'The Island'. In all, there are over eleven hundred entries.

This informative, attractively presented work, will be of interest to readers of this magazine and to anyone discovering Francis Brett Young, and getting 'hooked' - an excellent guide in how to proceed. To the growing band of aficionados, thanks to the efforts of the 30 year old Francis Brett Young Society, it is a mine of background information.

***The GWR at Stourbridge and the Black Country - The Life, The Times, The Men, Vol. 1*** by **Clive Butcher,** ISBN 0 85361 627 2, £14.95, 240 pages, published by The Oakwood Press

Following the success of his *Railways of Stourbridge* (1999), Clive Butcher continued his researches into the railways of the Black Country and this volume is the first of two, the second will be available by the time this magazine is published.

The longest chapter in Vol. 1 is devoted to a comprehensive account of railway workings from Stourbridge Junction from its opening in 1852 when there were six trains a day each way, three on Sundays, on a section of the OWW Railway. By 1867 the Stourbridge Extension to Handsworth was operative and the Stourbridge Town branch opened in 1879. The framework was then in place for a great expansion of passenger and freight traffic. Tickets issued in 1923 totalled 302,917 (365,636 from Cradley and Cradley Heath), and comparisons with recent passenger traffic are given. Parcels traffic figures for 1936 are given: 30,952 from Old Hill, 57,301 at Cradley and Cradley Heath, 23,733 at Lye. Workings at Stourbridge Junction marshalling yards and Stourbridge Town Goods branch are detailed and there are chapters on other local yards and the Halesowen branch.

Skilfully interwoven with the technical details, maps, diagrams and timetable extracts are some most interesting personal accounts of former railway men. The extent of stationmaster's responsibility beyond the platform surprised me. In the final chapter on the how the national rail strikes of 1911, 1919 and 1924 affected Stourbridge, the preamble lists the different grades of railwaymen which had their own organisations and whose rivalries sometimes impeded a common policy with which to take on the employers.

This is an essential book for all railway enthusiasts. For the general reader there is much to interest them in the personal accounts and in the photographs, scores of which are published here for the first time.

**SH**

*A rtists in Cameo Glass, incorporating Thomas Woodall's Memoirs* by H. Jack Haden, 52pp 7" x9.5" Price £4.95 (£3.95p to Society Members) Plus p & p from the Society.

This new publication by the Black Country Society includes several unique features. There are more than 20 illustrations, some full page, most of which are photographs by George Woodall. The author was instrumental in saving a large collectio of George Woodall's glass plate negatives, now at the Broadfield House Glass Museum, and those photographs included in this were developed by the late William F. Pardoe (authority on Witley Court) of Stourbridge.

ARTISTS IN CAMEO GLASS

Incorporating

Thomas Woodall's Memoirs

by

H. Jack Haden

THE BLACK COUNTRY SOCIETY
1985

In the extensive introduction and elsewhere in the book there are brief bigographies of several famous names in glass and notes on associated glassworks. The Portland Vase and its influence on Wordsley glass men and the Woodall brothers' work are covered in some detail. This is followed by Thomas's reminiscences reproduced in typescript, from his personal notebook. Thomas was an accomplished musician and his musical activities are covered. This is followed by his reminiscences about his work in glass.

Another feature of this most interesting book is the extensive set of references.

*A Black Country Voyage* by Peter Rhodes published by the *Express & Star* and the Black Country Society, ISBN 0 904015 73 4, 41 A4 pp including 25 in colour, price £3.99 post free to Society members from 57 Windsor Grove, Wordsley, Stourbridge, DY8 5AQ

This photo essay by the *Express & Star's* chief feature writer celebrates the West Midlands canal network. Hiring a forty-nine foot narrowboat, *Rosie*, from Penkridge on the Staffs. & Worcs. Canal, he and his 'First Mate' entered the north-western part of the Black Country.

When the voyage was made a year ago six daily dispatches from the correspondent reporting on his experiences as he journeyed appeared in the newspaper. After an uncomfortable first night and a ridiculously early alarm call ('torture of dawn chorus and church bells'), the inland sailors settled into a 4 miles an hour routine which enabled the diarist to pay close attention to aspects of the canal journey: water gypsies, the canal as a rubbish dump, escaping from alien forces, wild life and nearby hostelries and other attractions. Five days after entering the Black Country the escape was made via the Netherton Tunnel, Merry Hill and the Stourbridge 16 (locks) into the tranquil water of the Staffs. & Worcs. Canal at Stewponey, 24 miles south of the starting point. From here to the Bratch is one of the most attractive stretches yet in pre-James Watt days it was a hive of industry using the parallel Rivers Stour and Smestow for power. Peter Rhodes's sharp observations, with a touch of Jerome K. Jerome perhaps, illustrated by 25 striking colour photographs, make this a publication not to be missed - and look at the price!

*Foul Deeds & Suspicious Deaths Around the Black Country* by David J. Cox and Michael Pearson, ISBN 184563, 173 pp. pub. Wharncliffe Books in association with the Black Country Society, price £10.99.

The authors, previous editor and current editor of The Blackcountryman, David J. Cox and Michael Pearson, make an effective team to chronicle 16 crimes, the first in 1316, the last in 1943. In his doctoral studies, David Cox, a criminal justice historian at Keele University, has perused every copy of The Times from 1792 to the 1839, and several of the cases are of this period. Mike Pearson is a West Midlands Police Inspector and student of the Black Country's criminal history and is well able to compare police methods of the past with current practice.

I found particularly interesting the accounts about the deaths of the Gunpowder Plotters at Holbeache House, Wall Heath in 1605, the shocking police handling of the Wyrley Gang atrocities, 1903, and the intervention of Sir Arthur Conan Doyle to rectify the matter, and 'Bella in the Wych-Elm', Hagley 1943, the reporting and speculation about which, at the time, I remember.

It is surprising that throughout the period covered, careful records were made of serious crimes and the authors have made good use of these to present this fascinating collection of 16 of them covering cut-throats, traitors, rapists, thieves, murderous husbands and lovers, horse-slashers, torturers and thief-takers.

By arrangement with the publisher, Black Country Society members can obtain the book by sending a cheque for £8.99 (includes p & p) to Pen & Sword Books Ltd., 47 Church Street, Barnsley, South Yorks, S70 2AS, Tel: 01226 734555, Fax 01226 734438.

# Book Launch

*The beautifully restored Himley Hall was the venue on Saturday 29th July 1995 for the launch by Mr. Geoff Stevens of Jim Boulton's "Black Country Road Transport in Old Photographs" published by Messrs. Alan Sutton Publishing Limited.*

Over 150 people assembled to be welcomed by the Chairman of the Black Country Society who introduced Mr. Stevens, a son of one of the four founding brothers of the famous 1920s and 1930s motorcycle manufacturers, A.J.S. He described the book as excellent with the best reproduction of old photographs he had seen. He appealed to the audience to ensure that photographs in their own collections were clearly identified for the sake of future generations. He congratulated the author on sharing his expertise and enthusiasm with a wide audience and wished him every success with the book.

For an hour after the formalities the author signed over 70 books for purchasers and the Society served drinks and snacks. Many visitors also took the opportunity of buying items from the Society's stall, and viewed an exhibition in three other rooms by Dudley Society of Artists.

Several members bought vintage/veteran/specialist vehicles which assembled in the courtyard including two Clynos, two Lomax and an old scooter.

A review of "Black Country Road Transport in Old Photographs" by Cliff Webb, formerly Motoring Editor of The Times will be found on page 77.

*Jim Boulton signs Christine George's book while other purchasers queue for theirs to be signed.*

*Photo: Graham Beckley.*

# New Book Launch

**M**R. Charles Elwell, O.B.E. President of the Black Country Society, on Wednesday 29th September, launched a new Society publication, "Artists in Cameo Glass – Incorporating Thomas Woodall's Memoirs", by Stourbridge glass history authority, H. Jack Haden at the Kingswinford branch of the T.S.B. This venue was chosen as it was once the home of one of the cameo glass artists, George Woodall, featured in the book. George Woodall was also an expert photographer. Broadfield House Glass Museum has a collection of his glass plate negatives. Some 60 prints from these negatives were exhibited at the launch and 9 of them are included in the book. Corning Museum of Glass, New York, loaned colour transparencies for the cover illustrations. The other unique feature is the reproduction of Thomas Woodall's personal notebook about his life in the glass industry and music – he was a fine musician. This throws a new light on Thomas who is usually overshadowed by his better known brother George amongst glass enthusiasts.

The President launched the new publication by buying two copies himself and presenting one to the Deputy Mayor which the author signed.

*L to R: Lawrence Hollis (Chairman) Cllr. John Simpson (Deputy Mayor of Dudley)*
*Charles J. L. Elwell, O.B.E. (President) H. Jack Haden (Author) Stan Hill (Editor)*
*Photograph: R. G. Beckley.*

The Woodall family was represented by Mr. Wilday Allen, well known in Stourbridge, whose wife was descended from Thomas Woodall and Mrs. Jill Perry, a great grand-daughter of George Woodall.

The Deputy Mayor of Dudley, Councillor John Simpson, spoke of the importance of the Black Country and the Society's efforts over the past 26 years in helping to create interest in the past, present and future of the area. The Deputy

*'Intruders', signed by "T. & G. Woodall". Plaque 16½" in diameter. Made by Thomas Webb and Sons, 1894. Webb sale price £150. Four stages in its production are illustrated, Nos. 37, 38, 39 and 40, in "Nineteenth Century Cameo Glass." Pp 114, 115.*
*The above is one of the 18 illustrations in The Society's new publication.*

Mayoress in a descendant of Daniel Hancock who, at the Red House Glassworks, Wordsley, made the glass blank of the replica of the Roman Portland Vase which was sculpted by John Northwood c. 1876 giving an impetus to the rediscovered Roman art of cameo glass cutting.

Also in attendance were Mr. H. W. Woodward who as Brierley Hill Librarian (1939 to 1966) started the local glass collection, Mr. Roger Dodsworth, Curator of Broadfield House Glass Museum, representatives of the T.S.B., Lawrence Hollis (Society Chairman), Committee members, and representatives of the Black Country Society's Kingswinford and Wyre Forest Branches. Stan Hill, Editor of 'The Blackcountryman' who prepared the book for publication made the launch arrangements.

S.H.

## Appraisal of Two Novels by Local Author:
# Francis Brett Young - the Black Country's most famous author

### *The Iron Age*

The exploitation of the coal and ironstone which lay within the Black Country, and in the valley of the River Stour, the fireclay as well, peaked about 1860 when some third of the region's men were involved in its extraction and utilization.

The Iron Age focused on a substantial Stour Valley integrated firm, Willis, Hackett and Willis, an amalgamation of an ironworks, a colliery and a brickyard. Expansion came with the Franco-Prussian War of 1870-71 when both sides were supplied with iron goods.

Set in the pre-1914 years this was the first of Francis Brett Young's Black Country novels. Under the founder's son, Walter Willis, a remarried widower whose only son from his first marriage, Edward, is also in the business, the company drifts along, apparently quite comfortably, but in fact, towards bankruptcy. A brilliant engineer is engaged whose development of a special steel is seen by Walter as a lifeline to rejuvenate the firm.

Stafford, the engineer, tends to neglect his bored wife, and the solitary Edward completes the 'triangle'. This leads to serious consequences for the company with a possible different lifeline.

The author was born less than two miles from the novel's semi-rural setting and his grandfather was a director of the actual New British Ironworks on the site, and lived in Old Hawne Hall. The fine geographical and technical descriptions in the novel are authentic and the storyline is gripping.

### *Black Diamond*

This turn-of-the-century story starts in the Black Country and through its central figure, Abner Fellows, a miner and part-time footballer, drifts west to the mid-Welsh border country.

Abner's father was a tough, hard-drinking miner whose second wife was only slightly older than her stepson. Abner was found a surface job to ensure that a mining injury did not impede his footballing but when he refused to 'throw' a cup match for his boss, was sacked. His father was hospitalised at the time making Abner the breadwinner - he had a stepbrother - and things were difficult. Unjustly accused by his father of impropriety with his stepmother, a fight ensued, so Abner left home and tramped west. After several skirmishes he ends up lodging with a casual acquaintance.

By coincidence Abner again finds himself the breadwinner of another small family where the wife keeps him at arm's length. He works hard and fulfils a promise to the jailed husband, who is almost at the end of his sentence. The husband returns home, another fight ensues, Abner leaves, and in a drunken state a panacea is offered to him to solve all his 'women' problems.

With its infidelities, drunkenness, urban and rural poverty, violent death and explicit coverage of human frailties and desires, the book has all the ingredients for a 21st century best seller and was 'advanced' for its time. It is an absorbing tale with the characters well drawn, their circumstances accurately and sympathetically described reflecting the author's keen observation, shown also in the coverage of the workings of the law and its infrastructure, such as it was then.

This novel is in my 'Premiership League' of the author's many works.

# PUBLISHING:
The Black Country
Society's Association
with Alan Sutton
Publishing Ltd

www.suttonpublishing.co.uk

EARLY in 1994 an approach was made via the Director of the Black Country Museum to ascertain the possibility of finding authors to extend the publisher's range of books to cover more Black Country townships and interests. Society member Alex Chatwin was already involved as joint author of 'Bushbury in Old Photographs'. The publication of another book, 'Black Country Aviation'

84

by Alec Brew was imminent. Each author has to assemble about 250 photographs on his subject from which a final selection of about 220 is made, prepare descriptions of each and write an introduction.

The society committee agreed in principle to cooperate with the publisher and a meeting of potential authors with Simon Fletcher, Alan Sutton's senior commissioning editor, was held at the museum in May 1994. All who attended the meeting agreed to 'test the water' to see if the requisite number of photographs could be obtained.

Our proposal that any book published under this arrangement should carry the society's logo and also a statement about the society was accepted by the publisher and as there was just time to insert these into Alec Brew's Aviation book.

The first to meet the requirements was committee member Ian Bott, who, mainly from his own collection, had enough photographs on Wednesbury and being knowledgeable about his home town had no difficulty in writing the descriptions and an introduction. The preparatory work went ahead: 2 mock-ups of the book prepared, the descriptions typed up, page proofs corrected, amended page proofs checked and when publisher and author were satisfied a publication date was set. This was 10th November 1994 and the committee decided to hold a launch on Saturday 12th November at Wednesbury Art Gallery by kind permission of the director. Nearly 200 people attended during the morning and there were well over 100 there at the start to hear Lord Archer of Sandwell P.C., Q.C. launch the book. Books were sold and signed and the society also had a stall and provided the refreshments. By the end of the year 1,000 of this title had been sold.

The next book to be ready was Jim Boulton's 'Black Country Road Transport'. Ian Bott's experience was helpful to Jim who soon had 250 photographs for consideration from his own collection and from friends. A publication date was given and a launch was arranged at Himley Hall on Saturday 29th July 1995. Dudley Metropolitan Borough had spent £1.5 million renovating the building and we were fortunate to be able to hold the event there. Mr. Geoff Stevens, a son of one of the founding brothers of the famous firm A. J. S. launched the book before over 100 people and during the course of the morning over 200 attended. Several old cars assembled in the courtyard and the society provided refreshments and we had our own stall as usual. It was a glorious summer day and a bonus for visitors was that Dudley Society of Artists was holding the Summer Exhibition. Several of our visitors bought paintings.

Our next launch was of Trevor Genge's 'Sedgley & District in Old Photographs' on 30th September at Queen Victoria Primary School. Here before an audience of 120 Dr. John West, author of 'Village Records' and 'Town Records' and many books for teachers and pupils, launched his one time colleague's book. Both sales stalls and refreshments were arranged by society members.

After a two month respite we were into the book launch business again with three events on two consecutive Saturdays. On 2nd December at 11 a.m. about 60 people, mainly railway enthusiasts, gathered in the entrance of Hawthorns Stations on the new Jewellery Line for the launch of committee member Ned Williams's 'Black Country Railways' by the Mayor of Sandwell, Councillor Roger Horton, a railway enthusiast and member of the West Midland Passenger Transport Authority. We are grateful to CENTRO for obtaining the necessary authority for this unusual use of railway property.

By 2 p.m. many of those at The Hawthorns had made their way to Tipton Green Primary School where local interested folk had also gathered for the launch of 'Tipton in Old Photographs' by John Brimble and Keith Hodgkins , both former Society officers. The official launch was by former Society President Tom Brown, retired Headmaster of the school, who had trawled old log books to help him create a picture for us of the Tipton area in the period up to the earliest photograph in the book. This was followed by a slide presentation by Keith Hodgkins. Sales and signings followed and refreshments consumed.

The spate of launches ended with that for my 'Brierley Hill in Old Photographs' on 9th December at the Nine Locks Community Centre. Over 100 gathered to hear Mr. H. W. Woodward, who started the famous local glass collection when he was Brierley Hill's Chief Librarian, speak of his recollections of Brierley Hill before launching the book. Amongst those attending were the Bishop of Dudley and several local clergy who had been 'bribed' to attend by the author with the promise of an amusing story to be told about Anthony Whittaker and the Archbishop of Canterbury on his recent visit to the West Midlands. The event concluded with the sale of books and signing, our own stall sales and refreshments.

All of the books have done well. The Brierley Hill title became 'out of stock' 6 weeks after the launch (2,000 were printed). The society has benefitted greatly from this association with a national publisher with great experience in this field, 330 titles in the series having been published. We have had more coverage in the local press than ever, with the Express & Star being particularly supportive, and on local radio. Over 1,500 old photographs of the Black Country have been made easily available to the public and the society has benefitted so far by about £1,000 profit from our selling the books. Several more books are being prepared and some of these will be launched in 1996.

S.H.

*　*　*　*

Actress Josie Lawrence from Old Hill, previously best known for her amazing TV improvisations and comedy roles, has been recognised for her work as a classical actress. She has won the Dame Peggy Ashcroft prize for best actress in the Shakespeare Golden Globe awards for her performance as Kate in 'The Taming of the Shrew' at the Shakespeare Memorial Theatre, Stratford where she has lived for a year, together with her two cats, Aynuk and Ayli.

# 5.

# Black Country
# humour

As you know Stan has a predilection for wit and tales, which make him such a likeable bloke! Here is his lifetime's collection of Aynuk and Ayli stories, written by himself. Some are transposed from jokes heard or read in other parts of the British Isles, some told to him, some have come in moments of inspiration when out and about, monitoring current trends and events.

About 25 years ago Stan began a collaboration with his second-cousin Len Pardoe of Quarry Bank, former Able Seaman, Birmingham Evening Despatch cartoonist, Chad Valley Toy Company illustrator, and later on a freelance cartoonist with Leopard Press. Stan would supply the captions and Len would draw the cartoons.

When he asked Len to draw the cartoon for the Society's publication *More Black Country Humour, Tales and Verse,* it was the first one he had done for over five years.

Len's cartoons intersperse Stan's Aynuk and Ayli stories. Incidentally, Len, too had a pseudonym - 'Leopard' (LEOnard PARDoe), which he used when contributing freelance cartoons to other publications.

# Aynuk and Ayli shorts

Ayli told Aynuk that he had entered the pub's talent competition and would sing 'The Holy City'. He asked for advice on who should accompany him.
Aynuk: A bodyguard.

\* \* \*

On reaching his 100th birthday Ayli's grandad was asked how he was.
Grandad: Well, ah'm walkin' better than ah did 'undred 'ears agoo.

\* \* \*

On his first day at work at a filling station Aynuk was asked by a customer to check his tyres. In 10 seconds flat he was back and said, "Yoam alright mate, yoan got fower.

\* \* \*

Little Ayli on holiday at Blackpool was paddling in the sea in the company of another little chap who said, "Golly, your feet aint half dirty".
Little Ayli: Ah, well, we day cum on 'oliday last year.

\* \* \*

Trevor: Who cut your hair last time, your mother?
Little Aynuk: Yes, and she used a pudding basin.
Trevor: If she tries again tell her to use scissors.

\* \* \*

Ayli said that he now had a driving job in which he had no trouble with back seat drivers.
Aynuk: What sort of vehicle do you drive then?
Ayli: A hearse.

\* \* \*

Postman: I have a parcel here but the name on it is obiterated.
Aynuk: It ay fer me than, ma nairme's Aynuk Cartwright.

\* \* \*

Aynuk, Ayli and Lish, all a bit deaf, were walking round Greensforge;
Aynuk: Windy ay it?
Ayli: No it ay it's Thursday.
Lish: Ah, an ah bin, less all goo inter Ashwood Nurseries an' 'ave a cup o' tay.

0-0-0-0-0

Aynuk returned home early one night to find his wife in Ayli's arms.
Aynuk: Hey yoe, won yer think yoam dooen?
Mrs. Aynuk: There you are, I told you he's stupid.

0-0-0-0-0

New Landlord: You'll be perfectly at home here.
Ayli: Oh crtikey, ah came here for a good meal.

0-0-0-0-0

Applying for a job as a night watchman Aynuk told the gaffer he'd be perfect for the job as the slightest sound woke him up.

0-0-0-0-0

Young Ayli asked Aynuk for permission to marry his daughter Lizzie.
Aynuk: That's OK by me but an yer sid her mother yet?
Young Ayli: Oh ar, arn sid 'er but ah prfers Lozzie.

\* \* \* \*

*Preacher:  Have you found salvation?*
*Ayli:  Ah day know it 'ad bin lost.*

\* \* \* \*

*Vicar:  And will you love her, cherish her and keep her till death do you part?*
*Aynuk:  'Ere, 'ang on a bit vicar, ah oney promised ter marry 'er.*

\* \* \* \*

*Ayli:  Hey, Aynuk, yown gorra soup stain on yer westcut.*
*Aynuk:  No I ay, it's heggs.*

0-0-0-0

Census enumerator to Aynuk who was painting the front door:  Is the master of the house at home?
Aynuk:  Ar, 'ers down the garden feeding the chickens.

0-0-0-0

*Ayli had painful corns on both feet and went to see a chiropodist.  On entering the surgery he said, "Missus, ah'n brought yoe a 'ondful o' trouble".*

\* \* \* \*

*The doctor was called to Aynuk's sick bed and pronounced that he had not long to live. Aynuk's missus:  Doe lerrim goo yet doctor, 'e ay gid me this wick's 'ousekeepin' yet.*

0-0-0-0-0

Boss: I'm looking for a very, very careful, cautious driver for my Rolls-Royce.
Ayli: Ah'm yer mon.  Yoe con set me on straight away and pay me a wick in advance.

0-0-0-0-0

Aynuk: Ah thinken our little un 'as got ma brains.
Mrs. Aynuk: Ah thinken yoam right cuss ah've still got mine.

0-0-0-0-0

89

When little Aynuk did something clever Aynuk said to his wife: Ah think our Aynuk has got his brains from me.
Mrs. Aynuk: Ah knowen that - ah've still got mine.

o-o-o-o

Ayli: Wiers me glasses, ah wanten ter phone the bookie?
Aynuk: It ay yer glasses yoam wanten mate, it's a 'phone.

\* \* \* \*

Ayli: Me grandson's a gooen ter Iraq.
Aynuk: Thass a long way. How does he get there?
Ayli: Ah doe rightly know, but 'e 'as ter change at New Street.

\* \* \* \*

Aynuk was waiting under a canal bridge for his blind date to arrive when a very attractive blonde appeared.
Aynuk: Bin yoe Sarah-Jane?
Blonde: Bin yoe Aynuk?
Aynuk: Ar, ah bin.
Blonde: Well ah bay Sarah-Jane.

\* \* \* \*

Niece Lizzie: Uncle Ayli, ah wanten a mon. What sort of husband should ah look for?
Ayli: Now look 'ere ma wench. Yoe doe wan nobody's husband. Yoe goo an' find yerself a nice single feller.

o-o-o-o

Aynuk: Ay, yoe.
Ayli: Oom yoe a yoein'?
Aynuk: Ah'm a yoein yoe.

## Ode Aynuk says:

*Keep smiling, it makes everyone wonder what you are up to.*

Aynuk:   Is that the waiter company?
Operator: This is South Staffs Water plc, which department do you require?
Aynuk:   Tap wairter, please.

o-o-o-o

Operator: What is your address?
Ayli:    4B Court, Factory Road, Tipton.
Operator: Have you a code?
Ayli:    Now, ah all us spaken like this.

o-o-o-o

Gaffer:  Aynuk, yoam now 70. Yoan gorra think about retirin'. Yoan bin 'ere
         since yoe left school when yoe was 13.
Aynuk:   Now look 'ere gaffer. Ah ay ready ter goo yet. Ah should never a cum
         'ere in the fust plairce if ah'd thought it wore permanent.

o-o-o-o

In the Black Country it was found that the best way of keeping flies out of the
Kitchen was to have half a bucket of 'oss muck in the living room.

o-o-o-o

Aylis' uncle, a hypochondriac was only 39 years old when he died. On his deathbed
he gave instructions to his wife for his tombstone inscription to be: "Ah tode yer,
day I?"

o-o-o-o

Operator: What is your address?.
Aynuk:   177 Nanaimo Way, Kingswinford.
Operator: How do you spell Nanaimo?
Aynuk:   With letters.

o-o-o-o

BT operator on hearing heavy breathing: Caller, are you all right? Do you need
assistance?
Ayli:    No miss, ah'm all right. Ah ay got nerra pencil so ah'm breathin' on the
         winder an' when yoe giz me the number ah wanten ah con finger it on the
         misty pane.

o-o-o-o

Vicar:   How is it I haven't seen you in church lately Aynuk.
Aynuk:   Cuss ah ay bin!.

o-o-o-o

Modern dietary advice is that if you eat slowly you eat less. Members of large
Black Country families did not need experts to tell them that.

*    *    *    *

Ayli:    Missus, yower washin' 'as shrunk me shirt.
Missus:  'Ow much 'Olden's did yoe drink last night? Yoam tryin' ter get yer yed
         through the button hole.
*    *    *    *
Suggested name change for a store in Oldbury: 'Toys Bin We'.

*    *    *    *

A new nail shop has appeared in Cradley Heath High Street and has advertised for a nail
technician. The Chairman of our Industrial Archaeology branch has been informed.

91

Ayli:    Ah've just cum from our kid's funeral.
Aynuk:  Ah day know 'ee was jed.
Ayli:    ·They'm playen a dirty trick on 'im if 'ee ay.

o-o-o-o


Mrs Ayli: Every mornin', ah siz that new chap across the road kiss 'is missus as 'e leaves fer work. Now why cor yoe do that?
Ayli: Doe talk ser saft. 'Erd call the police. Ah doe even know 'er.

\*     \*     \*     \*

Aynuk: Ah con tell yoam a married mon. All yer buttons am sowed on perfectly.
New workmate: Oh ar. Sewin' buttons on was the fust thing 'er taught me after we got wed.

\*     \*     \*     \*

Ayli after dialling 999: Cum quick, me 'ouse is afire.
Operator: Keep calm. How do we get there?
Ayli: Yoan got one of them big red trucks ay yer? Well come in that.

\*     \*     \*     \*

Aynuk and Ayli were on opposite sides of the canal.
Aynuk: 'Ow did yoe get to the other side?
Ayli: That's a daft question ay it? Yoam already there.

\*     \*     \*     \*

Policeman: I shall have to have you locked up in a cell for the night.
Drunken Ayli: Woss the charge?
Policemen: There's no charge, it all comes out of the rates.

\*     \*     \*     \*

Gaffer:  Aynuk, stick this notice above the clocking-off machine. I con be sure then everybody siz it.

-o-o-o-o-o-

Teacher:    What is a monsoon?
Little Ayli: Miss, it's me big brother, cuss he'll be 21 in August so me dad says he'll be a mon soon.

-o-o-o-o-o-

Visitor:    Are those the local swimming baths?
Aynuk:     It depends where yoe liven, doe it?

-o-o-o-o-o-

Ayli:      Is this sirloin steak tender?
Butcher:   It is my friend. It is as tender as your missus's heart.
Ayli:      In that case, ah'd better tek two lamb chops instead.


\*     \*     \*     \*

Doctor:   Your husband will never work again.
Mrs Ayli: That'll cheer him up.

92

Aynuk: Why doe yoe ever 'ave a day off from work? Cor they do without yer?
Ayli: No, it ay that, it's just the opposite. Ah doe wanten 'em ter find out they could.

*    *    *    *

There's chaps where ah liven who woe work if there's a Sunday in the week.

-o-o-o-o-o-

Old Lizzie, a neighbour, asked Ayli if he would call at the post office to see if there was a parcel awaiting collection by her. She was disappointed when he called to say: Ar, it's thier all right.

-o-o-o-o-o-

Little Ayli: Ah've lost me dad.
Policeman: What's he like?
Little Ayli: Holden's Golden.

-o-o-o-o-o-

Mother: How is it I always catch yoe staelin' the jam?
Little Ayli: Iss cuss o' them soft slippers what yoam wearin.

-o-o-o-o-o-

Little Aynuk: Fairther, ah've just saved twenty pence by runnin' wum behind the school bus.
Aynuk: Why day yoe run wum behind a taxi an' yowd a saived a fiver?

-o-o-o-o-o-

American tourist staying at the Copthorne: We built the Empire State Building in New York in just 30 months. (Looking towards Merry Hill) By the way, what's that complex over there?
Ayli: Ah doe rightly know. It wor theer this morning.

*Ode Aynuk says:*

**"Unrequested and unwanted gifts always create the problem of acknowledgement."**

93

Aynuk: Did Edison mek the fust loudspeaker?
Henpecked Ayli: No, 'e day, but 'e did mek the fust one yoe could turn off!

-o-o-o-o-o-

The landlord pulled Aynuk a pint, strode over to the window, and, looking at the darkening sky, said, "Looks like rain."
Aynuk after taking a good gulp, replied "Ar, it tairsts like it an all."

\* \* \* \*

Vicar, just out of choir practice: Ayli, can you please supply me with a good treble?
Ayli: Certainly vicar, Cherry Nut, six to one; Roman Candle forty to one; Sunflower, eleven to two.

\* \* \* \*

Ayli: Drinkin' meks yo' look beautiful.
Sarah-Jane: Does it? Well ah ay bin drinken'.

-o-o-o-o-o-

Neighbours rushed round to Aynuk's house in response to terrifying screams and shouts of 'Murder'.
Mrs. Aynuk: It's OK ah'm oney tryin' ter wash little Aynuk's hair.

\* \* \* \*

Grandaughter visiting Ayli ill in bed: Ah've med yer a cuppa, 'ow many sugars dun yer 'ave?
Ayli: Doe ask me. yow'll atter ask yer gran.

## Ode Aynuk says:

*Synthetic yarn is what a Black Country mon tells his wife when he gets wum late.*

94

-o-o-o-o-o-

Dinner time school assistant to little Aynuk, who had that day returned to school after an absence: "Have you had chicken pox?"

Little Aynuk: "No missus, it was fish fingers an' chips today".

-o-o-o-o-o-

Doctor: "Does your husband take his medication religiously?"

Mrs. Aynuk: "He doe. Every time ah giz 'im 'is pills 'e cusses like a trooper".

-o-o-o-o-o-

Mrs. Ayli to neighbour: "Am yer gooen ter ode Lizzie's funeral?"

Neighbour: "No I ay. 'er woe cum ter mine".

-o-o-o-o-o-

Mrs. Aynuk: "Cum on Aynuk, weem gooen ter Sainsburys where ah con save 50% on Christmas presents".

Aynuk: "Ah knowen 'ow yoe con save 100%. Stop at wum an' doe buy any".

-o-o-o-o-o-

Teacher: What does God do?

Little Ayli: He sairves our gracious Queen.

-o-o-o-o-o-

Aynuk's factory was host to a visiting group of students from the engineering department of a local university. He said to the tutor, "We doe 'ave much educairtion round 'ere, we just av ter use our brairns."

\* \* \* \* \*

| Little Ayli: | Dad, will yer please 'elp me ter find the lowest common denominator out of this lot? |
| Ayli: | Well, ah goot. Ay they found that yet? Dun yoe know they was lookin' fer that when ah was at school 30 year agoo? |

\* \* \* \*

| Aynuk: | Ah've just cum back from Lisha's funeral. |
| Ayli: | Was it the beer what did fer 'im? |
| Aynuk: | No, it wor that. He drank a glass of varnish by mistake. He had a lovely finish. |

Aynuk: Sorry ter 'ear about yower missus bein' in 'ospital. It must be costing yoe a fortune.

Ayli: No it ay. It's all on the National Health, an' while 'ers in thier, er ay spendin' nothin'.

On his first day back visiting the Black Country from where he had emigrated to New Zealand 50 years ago, Tommy Bloomer met an old pal who said, "'Ow do Tummy, an yer bin on yer 'olidays?"

Soaked and fed up, Aynuk arrived home after an unsuccessful day's fishing in bad weather at the Fens Pool and announced, "Ah ay 'ad a bite all day'.

Missus: Yo' must be clammed ter jeth. Ah'll mek yer a bully beef butty.

Ayli: Drinkin' meks yo' look beautiful.
Sarah-Jane: Does it? Well ah ay bin drinken'.

Neighbours rushed round to Aynuk's house in response to terrifying screams and shouts of 'Murder'.

Mrs. Aynuk: It's OK ah'm oney tryin' ter wash little Aynuk's hair.

Aynuk: Ma missus is always unhappy when I ay with 'er.

Ayli: That's funny, ma missus doe trust me either.

Ayli: The doctor 'as tode me ter lose weight. He says that there's a very easy way ter do it. If yoe ayten slow, yoe aten less.

Aynuk: Well, yoe ood in our 'ouse 'cause there's ten of we.

A shopper went into a little shop kept by Ayli for a while and commented on the huge amount of salt he had in stock, packets from floor to ceiling on one side of the shop.

Shopper: Crikey, you don't half sell a lot of salt here.

Ayli: No we doe. We hardly sell any but the wholesaler's rep. does

Newspaper ad: 'CAR FOR SALE' - nearly new Astra, only 3,000 miles on clock, mostly done in search of a parking space at Russell's Hall Hospital.

# Aynuk and Ayli long-ens

A FAILING Black Country junior football team, The Wanderers, appointed Ayli as their new coach and he was dismayed when his new charges lost 10-0 to a local rival. Ayli rang up his old mate, Aynuk, who was the manager of a good team in a higher division and asked him how he should tackle his difficult task. Aynuk explained some of the activities in his coaching system: sprinting and relay games, set piece defending, corner taking and most important, dribbling. Aynuk explained that the latter included the use of 11 dustbins placed across the training ground, and the players were timed as they dribbled the ball round them from No.1 to No.11.

The new coach incorporated several of the suggestions and he was particularly keen about the dustbins idea. His team trained extensively for a week, and as there was no league fixture a friendly was arranged for the Saturday. On the following Monday morning Aynuk rang up his old pal to enquire how his team had fared after the extensive coaching.

Ayli: There was an improvement on the previous result. Wanderers 0 Dustbins 3.

\* \* \* \* \*

T HERE was a large attendance at the baptism of Ayli's grand daughter. The family gathered around the font and the vicar whispered to the baby's mother, "What's the baby's name?" He could not understand the reply and asked her to repeat it. She did so again in a slow, emphatic voice. The vicar nodded doubtfully. At the appropriate time he announced, "I name this child 'Spindonna'".

Later at the buffet in the Church Tavern, the vicar said to the baby's mother, "That is a most unusual name for your baby. I have never heard it before."

Ayli's daughter: When yor asked the nairm in the church, ah tode yer twice. Ah'd writ it on pairper an' ah'd pinned it on 'er, but yoe took no notice. Now look what 'er's struck with.

*Ode Aynuk says:*
*"A pessimist is a person*
*who complains of noise*
*when opportunity*
*knocks on his door."*

97

B LACK Country folks' helpfulness in whatever circumstances is legendary. There is a good example from an event in Paris last century when Aynuk and Ayli were members of their Wednesbury firm's contract team installing pipes. Ayli was arrested for brawling after he had been out on the wine one night, was charged and sentenced to death. Executions were public then, on the morning of the event a great crowd had assembled, as was the practice. The manacled prisoners were lined up to take their turn on the block. Ayli was third in line and watched the proceedings with great interest. The first victim was blindfolded and with his head on the block awaited the chop. The executioner pulled a lever and the crowd, at first silent, erupted with a great cheer when the blade stopped six inches above the victim's neck. As was the custom, the prisoner, to prolonged cheers, was freed. Number two was led to the scaffold and exactly the same thing happened.

Ayli had been watching carefully and said to an official, "Hey our kid, ah con see woss up wi' the mechanism o' yar big chopper. Yoe fetch me a ladder an' ah could fix it in two ticks".

Miraculously the lingo was understood and a ladder was produced. Ayli was released to climb it and after a couple of minutes fiddling at the top he came down and announced, "Iss OK now!"

Executioner (in French of course): Now we'll have number three.

•     •     •     •

*Aynuk the builder secured from the local Townswomen's Guild the contract to construct a rockery and garden on a spare piece of land by the church to commemorate the Queen's Golden Jubilee. He was several weeks late finishing the work but after much pressure he completed the job and an opening ceremony was arranged.*

*At the function the Townswomen's Guild was out in force and the Mayor made an appropriate speech. Aynuk was there in his best suit, accompanied by his wife wearing a big hat. He waited in vain for praise about his handiwork so he positioned himself near the door of the church hall and as the Guilders trooped in for refreshments he said to each one, "Ay yer glad iss dun?".*

*Each one gave him a stare and replied, "No I ay", and then an old lady followed and said, "Hey, I'm Gladys Dunn, what do you want?"*

•     •     •     •

Ode Aynuk says:

"Every family should
have 3 children then if
one is a genius the other
2 can support him."

98

Aynuk and Ayli were called to a house near the Whittimore fireclay pits where it was suspected that mining subsidence had cracked a sewer pipe. They dug down to the sewer and found that there was a crack in one length of pipe. Ayli was sent to fetch a replacement while Aynuk dug all round the six foot length in preparation to removing it. Ayli returned with the replacement in due course and was sent up to the householder to tell her not to 'pull the chain' for the next hour. Waiting a couple of minutes for him to deliver the message, Aynuk jumped down into the trench and started to remove the cracked pipe. Standing in the trench he had just prized the pipe away, when - WHOOSH - he was soaked from the open pipe from the house. Ayli returned, unconcerned.

Aynuk:    Ah tode yoe ter tell Mrs Chance not ter pull the chain, day I?

Ayli:      Ah, ah tode 'er. It wore Mrs Chance wot pulled the chain, it was me.

*    *    *    *

In the early 1920s a Black Country works football team was drawn away against a village team in a County Cup match. Their opponents' ground was carved out near the top of a landmark hill, 30 miles SW of their factory. The village team was well known for their 'physical' approach to the game. 20 minutes into the ball disappeared off the edge of the ground and down the hill, and several small boys ran down to retrieve it. This was convenient, for at that point five players, four visitors and one home player, were flat out on the grass from injuries. One by one the casualties raised themselves and both teams stood about impatiently waiting for play to be resumed. The ball boys puffing back up the hill delayed matters further by having a little game of their own and an impatient spectator shouted, "Never mind about the ball, gerron wi' the gairm"

-o-o-o-o-o-

In the early 1920s a Black Country works football team was drawn away against a village team in a County Cup match. Their opponents' ground was carved out near the top of a landmark hill, 30 miles SW of their factory. The village team was well known for their 'physical' approach to the game. 20 minutes into the ball disappeared off the edge of the ground and down the hill, and several small boys ran down to retrieve it. This was convenient, for at that point five players, four visitors and one home player, were flat out on the grass from injuries. One by one the casualties raised themselves and both teams stood about impatiently waiting for play to be resumed. The ball boys puffing back up the hill delayed matters further by having a little game of their own and an impatient spectator shouted, "Never mind about the ball, gerron wi' the gairm"

-o-o-o-o-o-

A priest, called upon at the last minute for a funeral because the local parson was indisposed, announced that he could not say anything about the deceased but if anyone present knew him and would like to say something, it would be welcomed.

After half a minute Ayli stood up and shouted, "His brother was wuss".

-o-o-o-o-o-

A wealthy self-made Black Country man was asked by a young man for his daughter's hand in matrimony.

Black Country man: Ood yer still luv 'er if 'er 'andn't gorra penny to 'er nairm?

Suitor: Ah, o' course ah ood, even though I ay managed ter gerra job miself yet.

Black Country man: Well, yo' con clear off, ween gorra nuff o' yower sort in the family aready.

99

AFTER a Saturday night drinking in Brierley Hill, finishing at the Bull & Bladder, Aynuk and Ayli missed the last 'bus (137 from Brum to Gornal Wood) home. Aynuk suggested that they walk to Harts Hill 'bus garage to see if they could borrow a 'bus to get home. They struggled up Mill Street, along the High Street and Dudley Road, which, as it was well past midnight, were deserted, and they found the garage in darkness. Ayli tried the gate to the forecourt and found it open.

Aynuk:      There ay nobody about. Less borrey a 'bus.
Ayli:       Con yer drive one?
Aynuk:      Ah con drive a lorry cor I? Iss oney like that. Yoe keep watch an ah'll get one out an' we con leave it in Zoar Street and walk the last bit.

Ayli kept watch anxiously. The only noises came from inside the gates: slamming of doors, revving of engines and other bangs. After about twenty minutes a single-decker came to a stop by the jumpy Ayli.

Ayli:       Won yer bin a doin'? Yoe ay arf bin a time.
Aynuk:      Yoe oodn't believe it. The daft beggars 'ad parked the 137 right at the back and ah 'ad ter shift fower other 'buses afore ah could get this un out.

*    *    *    *

Aynuk and Ayli were Cradley's night-soil men. One night they parked their cart outside No. 43 Stour Street, pushed their barrow down the entry and set to work emptying the cesspit. It was hot work so Ayli took off his jacket and hung it on the door to the pit which opened outwards. While they were emptying the first barrow load into the cart a gust of wind slammed the door shut, and when they returned they found that Ayli's jacket had fallen into the pit. Ayli lost no time fishing it out with his spade.

Aynuk:      Yoe ay goona wear that jacket now, bist?
Ayli:       Course I ay, not with it in that state but ah 'ad ter gerrit out cuss me sandwiches am in the pocket.

*    *    *    *

Ayli, doing a crossword: Wass the nairm o' monks wot doe spake?
Aynuk:      Thass easy - they'm called Trappists cuss they keepen their traps shut.
Ayli:       That fits if it's got two ts. Hey, ah wish ma missus ud join 'em.

*    *    *    *

Our two Black Country pals were dismayed when their traditional pub was taken over by a chain and given a refit. The new manager was sympathetic when Aynuk's grandson told him that the pals would not go again. He did not want to lose the custom of the area's champion drinkers, so he arranged for them to come for a special free trial meal and pint. The only item on the menu our two heroes could associate with was 'All day full English breakfast' so they opted for that even though they were invited to choose anything from the extensive list. When the excellent food was served the plates were overflowing with wum-cured bacon, wum-fed sausages, tomatoes, fried bread, brown hash, crusty new bread, accompanied by a pint of the guest wum-brewed.

Ayli was impressed and Aynuk was really but he did not say a word. When the manager enquired if everything was alright Aynuk said "No it ay. Ah doe liken yer wallpairper!"

*    *    *    *

Ayli: woz up wi' yoe, me ode mate?
Aynuk: Ah'm thinkin' ah've got typhoid fever.
Ayli: Ooo - that's serious. It either leaves yer jed or yoe endin' up a ravin' idiot. Ah knowen 'cause ah've 'ad it.

100

A T a local pub Aynuk ordered a plaice fillet and chips, and his huge wife a 16-oz T bone steak. A waitress brought these in and set them on the table.

Aynuk:    "Yoe ay goona ate that alone, bin yer?"

The Missus: "'Corse I ay, ah've ordered a big dish o' tairters an' mushey pays ter goo with it."

o-o-o-o-o

Mrs. Ayli:   "Ah was married in secret – even Ayli day know until he'd sobered up."

o-o-o-o-o

Aynuk won the local council's annual allotments competition and was presented with a silver cup. Interviewed by local radio he attributed his success to the extensive use of farmyard manure. In fact such was his enthusiasm for his methods that he used the word 'manure' 30 times. Listening in, his 18 year old daughter was very embarrassed and wondered what her new friends at college would think about her father's earthy talk.

Daughter:    "Mother, couldn't you get father to use the word 'fertiliser'?"

Mrs. Aynuk: "No chance. It's taken me thirty years to get him to use the word 'manure'."

o-o-o-o-o

Ayli: "Missus, pass me the Culture section o' the pairper, ah wanten ter see what time the wrestlin's on."

o-o-o-o-o

The favourite pastimes of Aynuk and Ayli were pigeon flying and fishing but they thought that they'd give snooker a try after watching a competition on TV. They went to a local snooker hall and after a few pints booked a table for the last 3 hours before closure. They had not got the hang of the rules and after two hours they had only potted the colours and couldn't seem to make any further progress.

Aynuk: "Look 'ere, we ay goona finish this gairm the rate weem gooen.
        Let's chate a bit an' tek the frairm from around the reds, we might 'ave a better chance then."

o-o-o-o-o

Stranger in Brierley Hill High Street: "Excuse me, could you please tell me if there is a B & Q in Brierley Hill?"

Ayli: "Ah doe know mate, but ah dun know that there's two Ds in Dudley."

o-o-o-o-o

New Teacher: "Everyone in this class who thinks that they're stupid, stand up." Nobody moved and after a few seconds she repeated the command. After another minute Little Aynuk stood up.

Teacher:     "So little Aynuk, you think that you are stupid do you?"

Little Aynuk: "No Miss, but ah feels so sorry for yoe stondin' up thier on yer own."

*Ode Aynuk says:*

*All too often the girl
who knows all the
answers is never asked.*

101

Aynuk: Which is more important, the sun or the moon?

Ayli: Well, it must be the moon 'and't it, cuss it giz us light when it's dark. The sun oney cums in the day an' iss light then anyroad.

\* \* \* \*

In the 1920s a bright young teacher from the south was appointed to a Black Country junior school. At the beginning of the half term before Christmas she was told of the traditional arrangements for the festivities on the last day before Christmas: each of the eight classes presented about 10 minutes of entertainment for the rest of the school in the 'drill hall' and then there was a brief Christmas talk by the Vicar before each class returned to their own room for their own class 'feast'. This consisted of an 'eats' bag with sandwich, cake, sweets, orange, apple and each pupil was given a small gift.

A week before the event the new teacher told little Aynuk that she had chosen him to say grace before the bags were opened. Little Aynuk was worried, he did not know what to say. He expressed concern and the teacher told him to say what his dad said before their family started their meals. The only time Little Aynuk sat down to eat with all his siblings was on a Saturday when his dad returned from work at 2 p.m. On other days it was a 'free for all'. He watched his dad carefully, paid attention to what he said and decided that that was easy enough.

Came the last day at school, the entertainment went well, the classes returned to their rooms 'raring to go'. The teacher called for order to allow Little Aynuk to say grace and he piped up in a loud confident manner: "Goo easy on the grorty pud 'cause iss gorra last fer Sunday as well."

\* \* \* \*

Ayli went to the local newspaper office to place a Death Notice for his recently deceased great uncle. The receptionist re-wrote his pencil-scribbled script and read it out to him for approval. On checking she told him that for the same money he could have another five words. He thought carefully and added to the revised script "Also whippet pup for sale."

\* \* \* \*

Aynuk and his missus had been watching the TV programme about the amateur opera sopranos who won the *Operatunity* contest. One of them whose partner supported her and her four children described him as her 'knight in shining armour'.

Aynuk: Yoe 'eard wot 'e said, ma wench, bin I yower knight in shining armour?

Missus (after much thought): Ar - ah supposing yoe bin, but yoe doe clane it very often.

\* \* \* \*

Aynuk: When ah gooen ter the new medical practice ah never siz the sairm doctor two visits runnin'. Ah preferred the ode way when yoe sid the sairm chap every time yoe went.

Ayli: Ah doe care who ah siz as long as ah gets me tablets. Any road, they all lernen it from the sairm book, doe they?

-o-o-o-o-o-

Aynuk and his grandson attended church together one Sunday morning and the lad was very interested in the plate being passed round during the final hymn. As it neared them he whispered to his grandfather, "Grampa, yoe doe atter pay fer me cuss I ay five yet."

102

From the Roman camp at Greensforge a troop of Roman soldiers was making its way towards Letocetum on Watling Street when passing through Bradley, near Bilston, there was heckling from a thicket near to the track: *"One Bradley bloke equals 10 Roman soldiers!"* The Roman commander stopped his column and ordered the first 10 men to get into the thicket and deal with the cheeky native. One by one the ten soldiers disappeared into the undergrowth and just as the last one went out of sight the first one came tumbling out of the thicket further along the track, without his armour or weapon. He was followed by 9 more, similarly disarmed, and the flabbergasted commander demanded an explanation. 10th soldier: *"You didn't say that there were two of them in there!"*

0-0-0-0-0

Aynuk went into a pet shop and asked the owner if he could buy a wasp.

Puzzled shopkeeper: *"A wasp? We doe sell wasps 'ere."*

Aynuk: *"Doe yer? Well, yoan got one in the winder."*

0-0-0-0-0

Henpecked Ayli on the 'phone: *"Doctor, mar missus has dislocated 'er jaw. If yoe 'appen ter be round this road in the next few wicks, yoe might drap in ter see 'er."*

0-0-0-0-0

Mrs Aynuk complained to Aynuk about always going to Blackpool on holiday. *"Why cor we goo ter Spain?"* she asked.

Aynuk: *"Hey, doe yoe be so dissatisfied. Ah looks after yer well, ah waits on yer ond an' foot, tecks yer down to Oxfam every month ter get a new dress an' yoe 'as a bottle of Guinness every night. Be satisfied. Yoam livin' the life of Riley."*

Mrs Aynuk: *"Ar, ah bin. Ode Mother Riley."*

0-0-0-0-0

Ayli: *"There's no doubt about it me ode mate, weem gerrin oder."*

Aynuk: *"Ar, an' it's a good job an all cus if we wore gerrin oder weed be jed."*

0-0-0-0-0

Young Aynuk was mending a fence when his pal young Ayli observed that he was throwing every other nail away.

Young Ayli: *"Why dun yer keep throwin' nails away?"*

Young Aynuk: *"Cuss the yeds am at the wrong end."*

Young Ayli: *"Well there's no need to waste them, just goo round ter thother side an' knock 'em in from thier."*

*Ode Aynuk says:*

*"Unrequested and unwanted gifts always create the problem of acknowledgement."*

103

Ayli: I 'eard a world famous brass band* at Dudley Town Hall last month.

Aynuk: Which one was that?

Ayli: Cor remember the nairme but their signature tune goos: "Wier an yer bin since ah sid yoe." **

Aynuk: Oh ah. Ah knowen the one. They 'ad a single in the charts 30 'ear agoo, "The Gornal Dance." ***

*Brighouse & Rastrick Band, **"On Ilkley Moor Bah Tat", ***"The Floral Dance".

-o-o-o-o-o-

Aynuk: Ma missus is always unhappy when I ay with 'er.

Ayli: That's funny, ma missus doe trust me either.

-o-o-o-o-o-

Lizzie: Wier an yer bin fer yer 'olidays?

Aggie: Fuerteventura.

Lizzie: Wier the 'eck is that?

Aggie: I ay gorra clue. We flew thier.

-o-o-o-o-o-

Ayli was leading his horse and cart when he was accosted by an enthusiastic election candidate looking for a photo opportunity, who gushingly admired the horse.

Ayli: Me an' this ode 'oss an bin workin' tergether fer nigh on 20 ear.

Candidate: I bet your employer treats you equally well.

Ayli: 'E doe arf. Last wick we wos both bad. Gaffer 'ad the vet ter th'oss and 'e gid me a wick off without pay!

-o-o-o-o-o-

Aynuk: It says in this geographical magazine that there's a plairce in Africa wier yoe con gerra wife for three pence.

Mrs. Aynuk: Why, that's terrible.

Aynuk: Oh - ah doe know, a good 'un ood be worth it.

-o-o-o-o-o-

Ayli: The doctor 'as tode me ter lose weight. He says that there's a very easy way ter do it. If yoe ayten slow, yoe aten less.

Aynuk: Well, yoe ood in our 'ouse 'cause there's ten of we.

-o-o-o-o-o-

A shopper went into a little shop kept by Ayli for a while and commented on the huge amount of salt he had in stock, packets from floor to ceiling on one side of the shop.

Shopper: Crikey, you don't half sell a lot of salt here.

Ayli: No we doe. We hardly sell any but the wholesaler's rep. does

-o-o-o-o-o-

Newspaper ad: 'CAR FOR SALE' - nearly new Astra, only 3,000 miles on clock, mostly done in search of a parking space at Russell's Hall Hospital.

104

Aynuk and Ayli were discussing the very cold weather experienced in early December last year:

Aynuk:     Ah sholl be glad when we stop gettin' them bitter winds cummin' straight over from the Russian Urinals.

Ayli:       Arr, an' me 'cause it ay oney the codeness, is it?

*     *     *     *

*The speaker's subject at the Sons of Rest one afternoon was "The Evils of Drink". He held up a glass containing water in which there was a worm which wriggled around. He then produced another glass and a small flask of whisky from which he measured about an inch into the empty glass. He then transferred the wriggling worm into the whisky which promptly dropped to the bottom, lifeless.*

Speaker:   *Now gentlemen, what does that tell us?*

Aynuk:     *If yoam sufferin' from worms drink plenty of whisky.*

*     *     *     *

The Parochial Church Council decided to replace the rickety coffin trolley before winter and heavy use and to approach local worthies to contribute towards the cost. Mr. Enoch, the Treasurer and local garage owner, reported that all whom he had approached had made a donation except the local doctor and it was decided that he should be asked again. The doctor was taken aback when asked and said, "Don't you remember, when I last paid you my petrol bill I told you to keep the change for the bier? I wondered why you replied, 'Well, thank you so very, very much doctor'".

*     *     *     *

*Ayli was repairing the gates of the cemetery one day when Aynuk approached him.*

Aynuk:     *Won yer recon yoam doin'?*

Ayli:       *Wastin' me time probably 'cause nobody out thier wants ter gerrin an' them wos in cor gerrout any rode.*

**Ode Aynuk says:**

*"The reason a dog has so many friends is that his tail wags instead of his tongue!"*

In the early 1920s a Black Country works football team was drawn away against a village team in a County Cup match. Their opponents' ground was carved out near the top of a landmark hill, 30 miles SW of their factory. The village team was well known for their 'physical' approach to the game. 20 minutes into the ball disappeared off the edge of the ground and down the hill, and several small boys ran down to retrieve it. This was convenient, for at that point five players, four visitors and one home player, were flat out on the grass from injuries. One by one the casualties raised themselves and both teams stood about impatiently waiting for play to be resumed. The ball boys puffing back up the hill delayed matters further by having a little game of their own and an impatient spectator shouted, "Never mind about the ball, gerron wi' the gairm"

-o-o-o-o-o-

A priest, called upon at the last minute for a funeral because the local parson was indisposed, announced that he could not say anything about the deceased but if anyone present knew him and would like to say something, it would be welcomed.

After half a minute Ayli stood up and shouted, "His brother was wuss".

-o-o-o-o-o-

Soaked and fed up, Aynuk arrived home after an unsuccessful day's fishing in bad weather at the Fens Pool and announced, "Ah ay 'ad a bite all day'.

Missus: Yo' must be clammed ter jeth. Ah'll mek yer a bully beef butty.

-o-o-o-o-o-

Ayli had been out of work for a long time and his wife decided that he should occupy himself with work about the house. They had a big Victorian style mangle in the brewuss and she decided that that could do with cleaning up.

Mrs. Ayli: Yo' con paint the mangle. There's several tins of paint in the attic'

After a few minutes there was a banging and thumping on the stairs.

Mrs. Ayli: Ayli, what the 'eck am year doin'?

Ayli: Gerrin the mangle up ter th'attic ter pairnt it like yo' sed.

o-o-o-o-o

Ayli's house was up for sale and the estate agent's advertisement description of it stated 'uninterrupted views for miles'. As there was a gasworks on one side, a foundry on the other, a graveyard on a bank next to the back garden and a big fence right opposite, the disappointed viewer asked about the uninterrupted views. Ayli: *"Try lookin' up."*

o-o-o-o-o

P.S. Ayli G. is not a Black Country mon.

o-o-o-o-o

Aynuk and his missus were having a meal at a restaurant on The Waterfront but the soup was so hot that he took to blowing it.

Mrs Aynuk: *"Behave yerself, yoe ay at wum now. If yer soup's too 'ot fan it wi' yer cap."*

o-o-o-o-o

On a 'bus in London Aynuk sat by a talkative Cockney.

Cockney: *"Ah fink we're in fer sum rhine."*

Aynuk: *"Dust?"*

Cockney: *"Nah, ah sed rhine. Look 'ew dark it's gone."*

Aynuk: *"I 'eard yer fust time an' ah said, 'Dust?'"*

Cockney: *"Ah said rhine an' ah mean rhine."*

106

All the Christmas presents were laid out on the floor in the living room and clumsy Ayli trod on the corner of a framed picture and cracked the glass. He was told sharply that he could get off to Wilkinsons as soon as they reopened after Christmas and buy a replacement. He did this and was quite pleased to find that the frame he was after was marked 'Two for the Price of One' so he paid up and returned home with two frames. Presenting them to his wife she said: "Wastin' yer money agen. Why an yer bought two frairms?"

Ayli: "Ah bought two in case the fust one wor the right size."

o-o-o-o-o

Aynuk to nephew who was just about to go out for his stag night: "Congratulations, young Ayli. This will be the happiest day of yer life."

Young Ayli: "But I ay gerrin married until termorrer."

Aynuk:     "Ar, ah knowen that."

-o-o-o-o-o-

Lizzie: Wier an yer bin fer yer 'olidays?

Aggie: Fuerteventura.

Lizzie: Wier the 'eck is that?

Aggie: I ay gorra clue. We flew thier.

-o-o-o-o-o-

Ayli was leading his horse and cart when he was accosted by an enthusiastic election candidate looking for a photo opportunity, who gushingly admired the horse.

Ayli: Me an' this ode 'oss an bin workin' tergether fer nigh on 20 ear.

Candidate: I bet your employer treats you equally well.

Ayli: 'E doe arf. Last wick we wos both bad. Gaffer 'ad the vet ter th'oss and 'e gid me a wick off without pay!

-o-o-o-o-o-

Aynuk: It says in this geographical magazine that there's a plairce in Africa wier yoe con gerra wife for three pence.

Mrs. Aynuk: Why, that's terrible.

Aynuk: Oh - ah doe know, a good 'un ood be worth it.

-o-o-o-o-o-

## Ode Aynuk says:

*Copper nitrate is the
pay policemen get for
night duty*

107

Aynuk was in the pub one Saturday night and on checking his lottery ticket numbers found that he was a winner. He jumped up and shouted, "Ah've won the lottery, ah've won the lottery," and charged off home shouting the same all the way there. He rushed in the house and the following ensued:

Breathless Aynuk: Pack yer bags quick, ah've won the lottery, quick, pack yer bags.
Mrs Aynuk: 'Ang on a minute, what for? We'erm we agooen, seaside or abroad?
Aynuk: Doe worry about that, just pack yer bags an' clear off.

*   *   *   *

Ayli: I 'eard a world famous brass band* at Dudley Town Hall last month.

Aynuk: Which one was that?

Ayli: Cor remember the nairme but their signature tune goos: "Wier an yer bin since ah sid yoe." **

Aynuk: Oh ah. Ah known the one. They 'ad a single in the charts 30 'ear agoo, "The Gornal Dance." ***

*Brighouse & Rastrick Band, **"On Ilkley Moor Bah Tat", ***"The Floral Dance".

-o-o-o-o-o-

Aynuk was in the bar when a chap with a Yorkie joined him and ordered a drink. As he did this the Yorkie cocked his leg up against Aynuk's foot and soaked the bottom of his trousers and sock. Aynuk did not say a word but just threw the dog a few crisps.

Dog owner: That's very kind of you considering what my dog has just done to your trousers.

Aynuk: Ar - an' when ah siz what end he picks 'em up with, ah sholl put ma boot up the other end.

*Ode Aynuk says, "A Black Country mon doe cry 'stinkin' fish'".*
*(See editorial).*

| Aynuk: | 'Ow's yer new job gooen at the factory. |
|---|---|
| Ayli: | I ay gooen back thier agen. |
| Aynuk: | Why not? |
| Ayli: | Lots of reasons: the sloppiness, the shoddy workmanship, the bad language, the bad time-keeping. They just woe put up with it any longer. |

\* \* \* \*

| Foreman: | When you recommended Aynuk for a job with me you said that he was a responsible worker. |
|---|---|
| Ayli: | That's right. When he worked with me he was responsible for all the trouble in the works. |

\* \* \* \*

**Aynuk stood for the council and when** out canvassing called on his pal.

| Aynuk: | **Ull yer vote fer me 'cause the council's full of 'jobs for the boys', bribery and generous perks.** |
|---|---|
| Ayli: | **And you want to put a stop to it?** |
| Aynuk: | **No, it ay that, ah wants** ter be part of it. |

-o-o-o-o-o-

There was a time when Worcestershire Country Cricket Club played occasional County matches at Dudley and at Stourbridge. On a visit by Kent to Stourbridge about 50 years ago, the visitors opened the batting and one of their openers, Colin Cowdrey, carried his bat and finished the innings with 165 not out.

Disgruntled Ayli: Ah'm thinkin' that beggar 'as played this gairn afore.

-o-o-o-o-o-

Aynuk and Ayli had been pals since Board School days. They had served in the South Staffs together during World War One and had worked in the same pit until they were in their seventies and could work no more. Their pleasure in summer was to go down to the park and watch the ducks. One day Ayli said, "Dun yoe know, although ween bin pals fer nearly seventy 'ear, ah cor remember yower fust nairm."

Aynuk, thought for a minute, and with his head on one side said, "'Ow quick dust want ter know?"

-o-o-o-o-o-

**Mother:** How is it I always catch yoe staelin' the jam?

**Little Ayli:** Iss cuss o' them soft slippers what yoam wearin.

-o-o-o-o-o-

**Little Aynuk:** Fairther, ah've just saved twenty pence by runnin' wum behind the school bus.

**Aynuk:** Why day yoe run wum behind a taxi an' yowd a saived a fiver?

-o-o-o-o-o-

**American tourist staying at the Copthorne:** We built the Empire State Building in New York in just 30 months. (Looking towards Merry Hill) By the way, what's that complex over there?

**Ayli:** Ah doe rightly know. It wor theer this morning.

109

A YLI was the only customer in the bar when two chaps went in and ordered two pints of bitter and two packets of crisps. The customer paid with a fiver and the manager first changed the note into five pound coins, rang up £3.40 in the till and from the change extracted coins for the crisps which he put into a tin at the side of the till and gave what remained to the customer. The customer watched this procedure and enquired if he always had to separate the beer from the crisps. Ayli came to the manager's rescue with, "Of course he does. Yoe doe want soggy crisps dun yer?"

\*    \*    \*    \*

Ode Aynuk and Ode Ayli were sitting in the lounge of their senior citzen's home on a very hot day when one of their fellow residents, Emmy Bloomer, said to her neighbour, "Ah'm so hot ah'm goon ter strip off an' walk round the pool." She did this and trotted without a stich on past Aynuk and Ayli and out into the grounds. After about five minutes Aynuk said, "Was that Emmy Bloomer wot just went past?"
Ayli:     Ah, it was.
Aynuk:  When'er comes back ah sholl tell 'er that 'er dress wants ironing.

o-o-o-o

Aynuk:  Whatever am yer gooen ter do when yoe retires? Yer werk is yer 'ole life.
Ayli:     Ah shull find plenty ter do.
Aynuk:  Such as?
Ayli:     Fer one thing ah sholl finish me book.
Aynuk:  Ah day know yoe was writtin a book.
Aylu:     Oh - ah ay rite in one, ah'm readin' one.

o-o-o-o

Staggering home one Friday night Ayli stumbled and bumped his head on a lamp post. A little later he stumbled into another, and then a third after which he decided to sit down on the ground and wait until the procession had passed in case he hurt somebody.

o-o-o-o

Aynuk's foreman in the brickyard annoyed him very much one day and he told Ayli about it.
Aynuk: Ah paid ode misery guts back though.
Ayli: 'Ow did yer do that then?
Aynuk: Ah pushed a barrow load of firebricks about all day but what the foreman day know was that it wa the same firebricks all day.

o-o-o-o-o

One Friday Aynuk found that there was as five pound note too much in his pay packet but he didn't mention it to the gaffer. However, the gaffer noted the mistake and the following Friday deducted five pounds from Aynuk's wages.
Aynuk: Hey, gaffer, ah'm a fiver short in me pay this wick.
Gaffer: Yoe day say nuthin' when yoe got a fiver too much last wick.
Aynuk: Ah con overlook one mistake but when it 'appens again it's time ah med a complaint.

\*    \*    \*

Ayli had been out of work for a long time and his wife decided that he should occupy himself with work about the house. They had a big Victorian style mangle in the brewuss and she decided that that could do with cleaning up.

Mrs. Ayli: Yo' con paint the mangle. There's several tins of paint in the attic'

After a few minutes there was a banging and thumping on the stairs.

Mrs. Ayli: Ayli, what the 'eck am year doin'?

Ayli: Gerrin the mangle up ter th'attic ter pairnt it like yo' sed.

o-o-o-o

At an annual Round Oak Steel Works Staff versus Workers cricket match on the works' ground off John Street the Managing Director was given out LBW on the last ball before the tea interval.

All the players and umpires made their way up the steps and past the bowling greens to the pavilion for the half hour tea break and on the way the MD still glowering about his dismissal said to a chap in a white coat, "I was never out LBW, You want your eyes testing."

Ayli (in a white coat) So dun yoe mate. Ah'm 'ere sellin' ice cream!

o-o-o-o

Newly married Aynuk was discussing married life with Ayli and said, "Ma missus is money mad." "Er asks me fer sum when ah wakes up, when ah cums wum for me dinner an' wen ah get wum at night. At wickends its wuss.

Ayli:      Well, woss 'er doin' with all this money?

Aynuk: Ah doe know. Ah ay gid 'er any yet.

o-o-o-o

Mrs. Ayli complained to her friend that her unemployed husband spent all his mornings in the pub, came home for an hour for his dinner and then went straight off to the pub again until turning-out time; only an hour at home on any day.

Mrs. Aynuk:    Well I am sorry to hear that.

Mrs. Ayli:    No need to feel sorry, that hour soon goes.

o-o-o-o

**Ode Aynuk says:**

*If yoe wanten ter get ter the top of an oak tree yoe con either climb it or sit on an acorn.*

111

Ayli complained that his missus put him up too few sandwiches to take to work so the next day she broke a large loaf into two and pressed in the middle the contents of a bully beef (corned beef) tin. On his return from work he complained that that day she had only given him one sandwich.

o-o-o-o

A gaffer was ready to pay a group of casual workers a pound a piece for the day's work when they refused to accept it saying that they had been promised thirty bob. They took a vote on it and eight raised their hand to object. The gaffer was encouraged to see one man did not raise his hand and said:, Will you accept a pound? He replied: Sure I'll accept a pound and quickly pocketed the pound note.

Gaffer: There you are. He's willing to accept my terms, so what about it?

Spokesman: Well he would wouldn't he. He's nothing to do with us. He's just come across from that path to see what all the noise is about.

*   *   *   *

Aynuk was hobbling about on crutches his foot heavily bandaged.

Ayli: Wos 'appened tey yoe our kid?

Aynuk: That fool in the overhead crane dropped a heavy sponner from 'is cabin on me yed.

Ayli: Well, why ay yer gooten yer yed bandaged?

Ayli: Oh, it day 'urt me yed, ah was wearin' me safety 'elmet, but ah was stondin' on a nail at the time.

*   *   *   *

Aynuk and Ayli were walking home along the canal towpath. When Aynuk reached home his wife said: Ah thought Ayli was with yoe. Wier is 'ee now?

Aynuk: Ah doe know. On the way wum he said the footpath was too muddy fer 'im and he was gooen ter walk in the 'oss road. Ah ay sid 'im since.

o-o-o-o

All evening Ayli had been ogling the new barmaid at The Four Furnaces. His wife, Mary Jane said that she had a nice bit of steak at home to put on his black eye.

Ayli: But I ay gorra black eye.

Mary Jane: We ay back wum yet.

o-o-o-o

At the end of their shift the men were putting on their coats but Ayli held back.

Aynuk: Cum on mate. Won yer angin' back for?

Ayli: Ah cor find me westcot.

Aynuk: Yoan gorrit on yer fule.

Ayli: So ah 'ave. If yoe 'ad'nt told me ah'd a gome wum we out it.

o-o-o-o-o

Gaffer at Ayli's retirement gathering: For 50 years Ayli has laboured at the most arduous, boring, physically demanding labouring on the site. He doesn't know the meaning of exhaustion, impossible, difficult, impracticable – so I've bought him a dictionary.

112

Soon after his golden wedding Aynuk's granddad died and all his relations said that it was a blessing as he had suffered 50 years of nagging from Liza Jane. For weeks after the funeral Liza Jane could not settle. She kept thinking of things that she should have reprimanded him for and hadn't, and on the advice of a friend sought a medium's help to make contact with the dear departed. This was duly arranged and the conversation went:

| | |
|---|---|
| Liza Jane: | Aynuk, bin yoe their? |
| Aynuk: | Ah, Liza Jane ah'm 'ere. |
| Liza Jane: | Ow bin yoe me mon? Bin um lookin' after yer aright? |
| Aynuk: | Oh ah. It's great 'ere an' ah'm very comfortable. |
| Liza Jane: | Bin yoe 'appier than wen yoe was wi' me? |
| Aynuk: | Oh ar, a lot more than when ah was wi' yoe. |
| Liza Jane: | Well, Aynuk, 'eaven must be a wonderful plairce. |
| Aynuk: | Oh – ah bay in 'eaven! |

o-o-o-o-o

*Emerging from the bookies Aynuk saw Ayli and said: 'Ah've 'ad a funny day in thier. Ah winnen one day an' losen the next'.*

*Ayli:*      *Well. Why doe yoe goo in every other day then?*

o-o-o-o-o

Ayli:      Hey, Aynuk, when ah was shavin' this mornin' ah noticed that me one eye's different from t'other.

Aynuk:      Which one?

o-o-o-o-o

*Visitor:*      *I say dear boy, do you know where a fellow might get a drink?*

*Aynuk:*      *No ah doe, but ah knowen where two chaps could gerra drink.*

o-o-o-o-o

# Ode Aynuk says:

*When a girl realises that she's not the only pebble on the beach she becomes a little bolder.*

113

Ayli took his eldest child, seven year old little Ayli, to the maternity unit to see the latest arrival in the family, the fifth girl. On the way there the little chap kept saying: 'Ah want ter see the stork, ah want ter see the stork.'

Ayli:          Ar, an' ah dun, ter ring 'is blinkin' neck!

0-0-0-0-0

*On a visit to a board school the Government inspector questioned a class of boys thus:*

*'Anyone shout out a number,' and a boy obliged with '67'. The inspector wrote on the blackboard '76', but there was no reaction at all from the class. He continued with numbers 84 and 25 and in chalking them up on the blackboard reversed them to 48 and 52. Still there was no immediate reaction but then Little Aynuk shouted 'Thirty three, now less see yer muck that about'.*

0-0-0-0-0

Ayli's *Express & Star* Golden Wedding tribute to his wife:

Aynuk/Liza Jane

50 years of love and argument

0-0-0-0-0

*After working late on a winter's night Ayli was driving behind a lorry which was obviously losing its load. He followed it along Wolverhampton Street and flashed the driver with no result. The lorry turned down the Himley Road and Ayli, intent on doing the driver a good turn, followed him and kept on flashing to the annoyance of the drivers coming in the other direction. At last he was able to overtake, slowed down and was able to stop the lorry driver.*

Ayli:          *Ah've bin tryin' ter tell yer yoam loosen yer load, our kid.*

Driver:        *Thanks mate, but this is a grittin' lorry, the forecast is snow durin' the night.*

\*   \*   \*   \*   \*

Aynuk: Con yer gimme the number of Ensnett Fish bar? Operator: Sorry - there's no listing. Have you got the spelling correct?
Aynuk: Well, it used to be called Pensnett Fish Bar but the 'P' fell off.

0-0-0-0-0

Ayli could not sleep one night and at 3am decided to give Aynuk a telephone call.
Ayli:   I 'ope I ay disturbin' yer.
Aynuk: No or kid, it's OK. I ad ter gerrup ter answer the 'phone.

0-0-0-0-0

Aynuk: Con yer gimme the number of the Woven Knitwear Company?
Operator: Woven? - are you sure that you have the correct name?
Aynuk: Oh ar - it's 'ere on me scarf, 'Woven in Scotland'.

0-0-0-0-0

Aynuk and Ayli had been apprehended by a policeman in the early hours and he questioned them: And where do you live?
Aynuk: No fixed abode.
Policeman to Ayli: So where do you live then?
Ayli: Ah'n gorra flat above 'im.

0-0-0-0-0

Ayli was on his way home late one night and as he had had a few was bold enough to take a short cut through the cemetery. Halfway through he heard cries for help coming from a grave, newly dug for an interment the following day.
Voice from the grave: 'elp me out, 'elp me out. It ay arf code down 'ere.
Curious, Ayli went to the edge of the excavation and peered down assessing the situation.
Ayli: Of course yow'm code, yer daft beggar, yo'an kicked all yer top covering off.

0-0-0-0-0

When Aynuk was foreman of Williams's Presswork Ltd. down the Level the manager told him that the owner's son was coming to help him during August and Aynuk was to see that he was made to think that he was useful. The lad turned up on the first Monday morning and reported for work. Aynuk was occupied making notes from the back page of *The Mirror.*
Aynuk: Ah'm busy at the moment so gerra hold on that broom thee-er and sweep down each

aisle between them machines.

Owner's son: But I'm a university student.

Aynuk: Oh, am yer now? Right, ah sholl atter cum an' show yer 'ow ter do it'.

o-o-o-o-o

Aynuk: Ay yoe.

Ayli: 'Oom yoe a yoin?

Aynuk: Ah'm a yoin' yoe.

o-o-o-o-o

Ayli: Is that South Staff Wairter plc?

Operator: Yes, which department do you want?

Ayli: Tap wairter please.

o-o-o-o-o

Caller to Jim Shelley (Black Country Personality No.52) on Carl Chinn's BBC Radio WM programme: Hallo Jim, I'm Charlie the tradesman who used to call on you. Have you still got that gondola in your garage?

Jim Shelley: Hallo Charlie, nice to hear from you. Yes, I've still got that conveyance in the garage but it's a Lagonda, not a gondola.

o-o-o-o-o

Little Aynuk at his cousin's wedding: Why is me cousin's bride dressed up like a dog's dinner?

Little Aynuk's mother: 'Cause it's the 'appiest day of 'er life'

Little Aynuk: Oh ar, is me cousin Turn dressed all in black then?

\* \* \* \* \*

Well-to-do Great Aunt Tilley (Matilda) was on a rare visit and seven year old little Aynuk's mom put on a special high tea in the front room in her honour. Little Aynuk stared at the old lady throughout the meal until at last Great Aunt Tilley said, "Little boy, why do you keep staring at me?"

Little Aynuk:     Ah'm waitin' fer yer ter do yer party trick.

Great Aunt Tilley:   And what might that be?

Little Aynuk:     Me fairther says yoe drinks like a fish.

o-o-o-o-o

Aynuk and Ayli were having a drink in the Saracen's Head when in popped a penguin from down the road, looked round the bar and said, "I've lost me brother. Has anybody seen him?"

Ayli:     Wos he look like mate?

o-o-o-o-o

Ayli's missus:    'Ope yoe wor insulted when Ayli walked out of church during yower sermon Vicar.

Vicar:      Well, it was a bit off-putting.

Ayli's missus:    It's nothing personal – he's bin sleepwalking since he was a child'

o-o-o-o-o

Aynuk: 'Ow's the missus me ode mate?

Ayli:   Same owd complaint, 'er's 'ad it ever since we got married.

Aynuk: Ah day know er'd bin bad all that time.

Ayli:   Oh ar, er's got I trouble - "I want this", "I want that", "I want that t'other".

o-o-o-o-o

Ayli is an avid watcher of TV 'soaps' but is tired of recent storylines and said to his wife: "Murder on Brookside, continuous bickering in Emmerdale, street fighting in Coronation Street, ankey-pankey in Eastenders; why cor they write a storyline about a normal couple like us?

Ayli's Missus:    Well, they an dun, it's on ternight at nine-o-clock.

115

Ayli:            What's that then?
Ayli's Missus:   One Foot in the Grave.

o-o-o-o-o

Aynuk was rushed to hospital for emergency treatment and it was nearly two weeks before he was well enough to be sent home. After another week Ayli visited him and enquired if Aynuk's own doctor was keeping an eye on him.
Aynuk:   Oh, 'e ay bin yet but he's sent me a get well card.

o-o-o-o-o

Ayli did not call for Aynuk to go to work one morning so the latter, hearing a lot of banging in his friend's back yard next door, jumped on a box to look over the fence to see what was going on and said, "Ay yoe cummin ter werk terday?"
Aynuk:   "No our kid. Ma missus ay arf bad with the 'flu", whereupon Mrs. Aynuk had an almighty coughing fit in their back kitchen.
Ayli:    Is that 'er coughin'?
Aynuk:   No yer fule. 'Ers 17 stoon. This 'oodn't be big enough fer 'er, ah'm
         mekkin a box fer our grandson's 'amster.

o-o-o-o-o

Little Aynuk's sister:   'Ow did mother know yoe day 'ave a bath?
Little Aynuk:            Ah forgot ter wet the soap.

o-o-o-o-o

Aynuk:   So yoam goona marry Wider Bloomer. Ah ood'nt like ter be the second
         'usband of a wider.
Ayli:    Its better than being the fust.

*Ode Aynuk says:*

*The biggest room in the world is room for improvement.*

116

| | |
|---|---|
| Aynuk dialled 999: | Cum quick, me missus wor gerrup, 'er might be jed. |
| Operator: | Address please caller. |
| Aynuk: | 177B Nanaimo Road. |
| Operator: | Please spell that. |
| Operator after pause: | Caller, are you still there? Please spell out your address. |
| Aynuk: | Look, ah'll drag 'er on to Bromley Lane an' yoe con pick 'er up thier – B-R-O-M-L-E-Y. |

o-o-o-o-o

| | |
|---|---|
| Ayli's Missus: | 'Ow much ter sole an' 'eel; this pair o' shoes? |
| Cobbler: | 7/6d sole, 2/6d heel. |
| Ayli's Missus: | Right, yoe con 'eel 'em all over. |

o-o-o-o-o

| | |
|---|---|
| Aynuk's Missus: | Ah day like the sermon, ah day like the organ music, the sates am uncomfortable and the church was code. |
| Sidesman who took the collection: | Well, what do you expect for a penny? |

o-o-o-o-o

A chap walked into a pub very awkwardly with his head at an angle of 45 degrees and asked for a pint of best bitter. The landlord duly obliged and the drinker, with some difficulty lifted the glass to his lips and took a great swig spilling some beer down his front.

| | |
|---|---|
| Landlord: | That will be £1.60p please. |
| Drinker: | I ay got no money. |
| Landlord: | You cheeky beggar. If yowd played that trick at the Four Furnaces just up the road the 20 stoon gaffer thier ood 'ave broken yer blinkin' neck. |
| Drinker: | Ah've just cum from the Four Furnaces. |

o-o-o-o-o

| | |
|---|---|
| Telephone caller just before the election: | This is a telephone poll. |
| Ayli: | Oh ar, an' this is a lamp post. |

o-o-o-o-o

| | |
|---|---|
| Aynuk: | We 'ad 9 kids in our family an' we wus so poor we were fed mainly on Windmill Pie. |
| Ayli: | Wos Windmill Pie, ah ay never 'ad none o' that? |
| Aynuk: | Its in a big dish an' yoe grabs a bit as it goos round. |

o-o-o-o-o

Ayli's missus told Aynuk's missus that Ayli had been knocking her about.

| | |
|---|---|
| Ayli's Missus: | When he comes out ah'm goona sue 'im fer divorce. |
| Aynuk's Missus: | Cums out, where is 'e then? |
| Ayli's Missus: | 'E's in 'ospital. |

o-o-o-o-o

Aynuk and Ayli were watching the 2004 European Cup Final when there was a considerable delay.

| | |
|---|---|
| Ayli: | Wos the 'old up? The referee is only bookin' somebody. |
| Aynuk: | Ar he is, but an yer sid the length o' them Greek chaps' nairms? |

117

Aynuk to pub landlord: Our pigeon flying club wants to hold a bit of a do. Con we 'ave a room please?

Landlord:  If there's fewer than fifty you can have the room free. If there's more than that you'll need the bigger room and there's a charge for that. How many are you expecting?

Aynuk:  Forty nine and a half!

\*   \*   \*   \*

Old Ayli had a good funeral and was buried in the family tomb at St. Luke's. Aynuk was concerned that the headstone was leaning at an angle and next day decided to try and straighten it up. He could not get it to stay in position so went home to find some rope to pull it upright. He found some stout cable, returned with that and tied it round the headstone and the other end round a tree branch and heaved to get it vertical. He went home again to get some rubble to pack in at the base and while he was away the grieving widow, accompanied by a friend, attended to tidy up the floral tributes.

Ayli's widow: Look at that. Ah cor believe it. 'Ee's oney bin down thier a day an' 'ee's got the 'phone in aready!

\*   \*   \*   \*

Young Ayli, a miner, took his young bride-to-be to a Dudley jeweller's shop to choose a ring and asked to see some.

Jeweller:  Eighteen carat?

Young Ayli: No mate, chewin' bacca, now less see the rings.

\*   \*   \*   \*

The two Black Country pals visited the motor show at the NEC, and walked through an area packed with vehicles.

Ayli:  Ah doe think much o' them. Yoe con see the sairm every day at Merry Hill.

Aynuk:  Ode on, reserve judgement. We ay bin in yet. This is the car park.

\*   \*   \*   \*

Ayli's grandson was helping him in the garden.

Ayli:  That rake ay the tool fer the job. Use this one. Dun yer know what it is? It is a hoe.

Grandson:  Fairther Christmas has got three o' them, 'cause last time ah sid 'im at Rackham's, 'e said, " Ho, ho, ho, little boy".

*Ode Aynuk says:*
*(with reference to school tests)*

*"Yoe doe mek a pig heavier by keep weighing it"*

In a raffle Aynuk's missus won a year's membership of an expensive health club and attended regularly. After three months she told her husband how pleased she was with her progress, "My personal trainer says I've a face like an 18 year old and a figure of a 21 year old."

Aynuk: Oh ar. An' what did 'e say about yer 50 year old bum?

Aynuk's missus: In all the three months ah've known 'im 'e day mention yoe once.

o-o-o-o

A vicar who was leaving his parish paid a farewell visit to Ayli's great grand father, his oldest parishioner. The old man shook the vicar's hand warmly and said, "Yower replacement woe be as good as yown bin".

Vicar: That's rubbish, but I am very flattered.

Old man: It's true. Ah've bin 'ere under five vicars an' each one 'as bin wuss than the last.

o-o-o-o

Aynuk was taking delivery of a parcel for his gaffer and the blunt pencil which he used to sign for it did not make an impression through the carbon paper.

Carter: Put your weight on it.

Aynuk wrote: 11st. 2lbs.

o-o-o-o

Ayli's missus to her husband: What ood yer like me ter buy yer this 'ear fer Christmas?

Ayli: Yoe con gee it a miss this 'ear as ah cor afford it.

o-o-o-o

Aynuk had an eye infection and part of the treatment was to bathe it in warm water twice a day.

Ayli: 'Ow's yer eye now?

Aynuk: It must be better, ah've bin bathin' the wrong un fer a fortnet.

o-o-o-o

Election candidate: Can you hear me at the back?

Ayli: Ar, ah con but ah oodn't mind changin' sates wi' somebody oo cor.

o-o-o-o

Bishop: Who is this who sees all, hears all and before whom even I am a crushed worm?

Aynuk: Yer missus, me Lord.

o-o-o-o

Ayli opened up his mantlepiece clock to see why it wasn't working. On finding a dead beetle within he said, "No wonder it owe goo, the blinkin' driver's jed".

o-o-o-o

Aynuk declared a batsman not out even though he was well out of his crease when the wicket was broken.

Bystander: 'Ow cor 'e be out when 'e was half way down the wicket?

Aynuk: Cus ah wor lookin', that's why.

119

Aynuk's foreman in the brickyard annoyed him very much one day and he told Ayli about it.

Aynuk: Ah paid ode misery guts back though.

Ayli: 'Ow did yer do that then?

Aynuk: Ah pushed a barrow load of firebricks about all day but what the foreman day know was that it wa the same firebricks all day.

o-o-o-o-o

Boss: I'm looking for a very, very careful, cautious driver for my Rolls-Royce.

Ayli: Ah'm yer mon. Yoe con set me on straight away and pay me a wick in advance.

o-o-o-o-o

Aynuk: Ah thinken our little un 'as got ma brains.

Mrs. Aynuk: Ah thinken yoam right cuss ah've still got mine.

o-o-o-o-o

Tight fisted Ayli decided to hold a party in his flat. Aynuk asked if his cousin could attend and Ayli explained to him how to get there.

Ayli: Ah'm on the 6th flewer of Northwood Court. Cum up in the lift an' press the bell on No. 4 with your elbow and as the dooer opens gee it a kick.

Aynuk's cousin: Why use my elbow and foot?

Ayli: Well yoe ay cummin empty onded bin yer?

o-o-o-o-o

Aynuk returned home early one night to find his wife in Ayli's arms.

Aynuk: Hey yoe, won yer think yoam dooen?

Mrs. Aynuk: There you are, I told you he's stupid.

o-o-o-o-o

New Landlord: You'll be perfectly at home here.

Ayli: Oh crtikey, ah came here for a good meal.

o-o-o-o-o

Applying for a job as a night watchman Aynuk told the gaffer he'd be perfect for the job as the slightest sound woke him up.

o-o-o-o-o

Young Ayli asked Aynuk for permission to marry his daughter Lizzie.

Aynuk: That's OK by me but an yer sid her mother yet?

Young Ayli: Oh ar, arn sid 'er but ah prfers Lozzie.

o-o-o-o-o

After little Aynuk's baptism the vicar was filling the register 'Aynuk Homer Bloomer' when he came to the second Christian name.

Vicar: Aynuk, what an interesting choice of name. Is 'Homer' after your favoutite Greek poet?

Aynuk: Poet? No, no, no, ah'm a pigeon flier.

o-o-o-o-o

Gaffer at Ayli's retirement gathering: For 50 years Ayli has laboured at the most arduous, boring, physically demanding labouring on the site. He doesn't know the meaning of exhaustion, impossible, difficult, impracticable – so I've bought him a dictionary.

120

Aynuk's granddad was advised not to keep all of his money in the house and was persuaded to deposit his savings in the newly opened branch of a major bank opposite his cottage. He carried a bucket full of gold sovereigns there one day, tipped them before a clerk and said, "Count that lot." After some time the clerk said, "£835 in gold coins."

Granddad: That ay right, count 'em agen.

Clerk, after a recount: Forty-one piles of twenty coins, that's £820, and fifteen in addition. That's £835.

Granddad: Crikey, ah must 'ave brought the wrong bucket. Tip em all back an' ah'll goo an' fetch the right one.

o-o-o-o-o

Ayli studied the prices board at a local fish and chip shop. The fish was £2.80 and the chips either 90p or 60p.

Ayli:      Ah'll just 'ave a bag o' chips please.

Demetrios: 90 or 60?

Ayli:      If yoam a gooen ter count 'em, doe bother.

o-o-o-o-o

Aynuk:     Ah bought ma missus a ball pint pen fer 'er birthday.

Ayli:      Was 'er plaised?

Aynuk:     Naw, 'Er wos expectin' a washin' machine.

o-o-o-o-o

Ayli:      Won yer think o' the gairm yesterday?

Aynuk:     Well, ah day expect our lot ter get 'ommered twenty ter nothin' but when it got ter thirteen nothing summat tode me we wos in fer an 'idin'.

o-o-o-o-o

Little Aynuk's mum:  Why 'as yower taicher put the naughtiest boy in the school ter sit next ter yoe?

Little Aynuk:  'Er thinks ah sholl be a good influence on 'im. Thass all 'er knows. Ah con teach 'im a few tricks.

**Aynuk says:**

*"It is better to remain silent and appear a fool than to speak and remove all doubt".*

Ayli's Missus: Hey Ayli, thay'n got half-priced suits at Merry Hill's Debenhams next wick. Now it's our Ruby Wedding soon. Ood yoe like a new suit fer the occasion?

Ayli: Ah doe want a new suit. I 'ad one when we got married day I?

o-o-o-o-o

Four-year-old Aynuk went with his mother to a ladies' sauna at the local fitness centre one day where she deposited him in the crèche and then disappeared to 'sweat it off'. Aynuk became bored and managed to slip his minder and luckily managed to find the drying room door, opened it and wandered in. Several ladies had just emerged from the steam, saw little Aynuk and started to scream as they rushed to find a towel.

Little Aynuk: Wos up wi' yoe lot, ay yoe never sid a little chap afore, where's me muther?

* * * * *

Aynuk's old banger was run into by a big car driven by a very posh chap who apologised most profusely and said, "It was an Act of God".

Aynuk: Yoe fancy yerself, doe yer?

* * * *

*Little Ayli when taking a Scout first aid test was asked what he'd do if his little brother swallowed the house key.*

*Little Ayli: Climb through the winder.*

* * * *

Aynuk, a keen pigeon fancier, took a stranger he'd met in the pub to see his pigeons.

Visitor: That's a fine pigeon on the roof.

Aynuk: That ay a pigeon, it's a gull off the council tip.

Visitor: Whether it's a gull or a boy, it is still a fine pigeon.

* * * *

*The scripture teacher described what a wonderful place heaven is and asked her class who wanted to go there. All except little Ayli put up their hands.*

*Teacher: Now Ayli, why don't you want to go to heaven?*

*Little Ayli: Well miss, ah'd like to but me fairther tode me ter goo straight wum after school.*

# ...and finally

# *Anthony and the Archbishop*

ANTHONY Whittaker started his working life in E. J. & J. Pearson's brickyard but its closure and his loss of a job set him on path to becoming a very successful businessman. Along the road he bought the site of the old Brierley Hill gasworks and converted it into a trading estate with about 100 units there. He would have liked to be an RAF pilot but did not have the opportunity but he has been able to satisfy his desire to fly by owning a helicopter, and according to his

122

Civil Aviation Authority supervisor, has become a superb pilot. He also owns a Rolls-Royce limousine.

Anthony's success has been recorded in 'The Blackcountryman' (Vol. 25 No. 1). He is well known in the area for supporting good causes and knowing this the Vicar of Quarry Bank called upon him to help out in an emergency which has arisen in connection with the visit of the Archbishop of Canterbury to the West Midlands in Autumn 1995. The timetable difficulty was overcome with Anthony agreeing to fly the Archbishop from London to his first appointment at Malvern. There for local engagements Anthony' son was waiting with the Rolls-Royce. The Archbishop stayed with the Bishop of Worcester at Hartlebury Castle from where a visit to Castle High School, Dudley was made.

On the day of departure the Archbishop needed to get to Birmingham Airport and Anthony, attired in his best suit, collected him from Hartlebury and was soon on the M42. After 5 minutes on the motorway the Archbishop remarked that it has been a boyhood ambition to drive a 'roller' and could he have a go at the wheel. Anthony agreed, pulled onto the hard shoulder and changed places with the Archbishop.

The new driver put his foot down and soon they were travelling at 120 mph. After 5 miles a police car siren was heard and they were pulled over by the local force's recently acquired souped up Skoda and the following conversation ensued:

Patrolman: Excuse me sir, you have been travelling at 120 mph. Wait here while I radio HQ.

Patrolman: Serg. I have just stopped a Roller doing 120 mph.

Sergeant: Book him.

Patrolman: Hang on a minute, he looks very important. Do you think I should. We do not want any repercussions.

Sergeant: How important, is he more important than me?

Patrolman: Oh ah, he's more important than you.

Sergeant: Is he more important than the Chief Inspector?

Patrolman: I'd say he is much more important than the Chief Constable.

Sergeant: Well, what makes you think he's more important than the Chief Constable.

Patrolman: Well Sergeant he must be 'cause he's got the Archbishop of Canterbury as his chauffeur.

(Some of this story is true. The reader is left to decide at what point it turns to fiction).

# Index

126

Lightning Source UK Ltd.
Milton Keynes UK
06 September 2009
143368UK00001B/100/P